Your Astrological Health

a guide for daily living

Christina Richter

Disclaimer

The information in this book is for educational purposes only. The content herein is NOT medical advice, diagnosis or prescription. In seeking healing solutions, it is strongly advised that you work with qualified practitioners in the respective field.

Please note: It is recommended to seek professional advice from the appropriate practitioner if you wish to use herbs as part of your lifestyle as some herbs interact with prescribed medications.

The author is not responsible for damage and other liabilities.

All rights reserved. No part of this book may be replicated mechanically, photographically, or electronically, or in the form of a phonographic recording; nor may it be stored, transmitted or otherwise be copied for public or private use, other than for "reasonable use" as brief quotations embodied in articles and reviews, without the prior written permission of the author.

The moral rights of the author have been asserted.

Copyright © Christina Richter, 2020

Published by White Light Publishing House 2020

ISBN 978-0-6487529-6-7

Think outside the box, look to the heavens for insight

and you will always have options.

Christina Richter

To all those people who choose the path of physical, emotional and spiritual health.

This book is dedicated to you.

Contents

Foreword	1
Introduction	3
How to use this book	7
The Signs of the Zodiac	9
Aries	13
Taurus	22
Gemini	31
Cancer	39
Leo	48
Virgo	56
Libra	64
Scorpio	73
Sagittarius	82
Capricorn	91
Aquarius	100
Pisces	109
For the Advanced Astrologer	117
Acknowledgments	148

Foreword

Christina is proving herself to be one of the more qualified and experienced Astrologers. Her skill is being able to pen solutions so profoundly but in simple terms that we can all understand. Christina's Nursing experience shines through, along with decades of study into the medical side of the planets, going right back to, and including the older art of Healing; Ayurveda, Plants, and Moon cycles, that all play an important part in self-awareness of your body.

Christina's recommended practice is not a complicated system to integrate into your own life and bookshelf; Christina's 3rd book continues the Journey to that Awareness and Healing of SELF.

I have had the pleasure of working with Christina over the last few years, and we continue to brainstorm ways to 'Teach what we know' for your personal satisfaction and knowledge of embracing the Whole-istic way of Life.

Our spiritual, emotional, psychological, mental, and psychical body all need to be in alignment with our soul contract, the 'blueprint' of our own journey. Life as we know it in today's busy world does have its challenges, so this book is vital to help you keep the balance between yourself, and what life expects of you.

Kath Tutill
Professional Astrological Counsellor Q.B.E.
Former President for 6 years of the Astrology Foundation Inc.
(AFI) Auckland, New Zealand
AFI Committee member and Conference coordinator

www.astrologyfoundation.co.nz

Introduction

Welcome to my new book *Your Astrological Health, a guide for daily living*. As I had such good feedback on my first book. *Learn to Self Heal*, I was inspired to write this follow up book.

So here it is. This book can be used independently or in conjunction with *Learn to Self Heal,* and you do not need to be an astrologer to understand this book. As stated in my first book, I offer of a FREE astrology chart. Email me at crscorpio1111@gmail.com with your date, time and city of birth or go to www.astro.com and follow the guidelines for a free chart.

For those of you who are reading me for the first time, let me introduce myself. I am a full-time practising Holistic Astrological Consultant, specialising in Medical Astrology. My 35-year background as a Registered Nurse (mainly in Intensive Care), Ayurveda, Colour Therapy, Healing Touch and Stress Management have given me experience and insights to other people's perceptions to do with health and disease. My personal journey with potentially major health dilemmas, guided me to seek out alternatives that avoided surgery.

Recently I was suffering with body weakness and bone loss: e.g. my tooth fell out for no apparent reason; forgetfulness, brain fog and I needed to sleep in the afternoon. My symptoms were vague and non-specific and could not be related to any condition, but I knew something was wrong. My Holistic Doctor recommended a specific blood test that came back with a very low level of Vitamin D. My only other indicator was a slightly high reading of my parathyroid gland, all other blood tests were normal. I was diagnosed with hyperparathyroidism with surgery my only cure. With my belief that you can prevent surgery (not in traumatic or life-threatening cases), I did a deal with my Doctor. I said, "*Give me 6 months to see if I can bring my blood level down to normal. If I am not successful, I will agree to the surgery*". He agreed and my challenge started.

First, I looked at my astrology chart to see if it revealed indications of what I was experiencing in my body. I looked for Vitamin D deficiency. In Astrology Vitamin D is ruled by your Sun sign which is indicated by the day you were born. My Sun sign is in Scorpio in the element of water. After analysis of my transits, progressions, and the condition of my Sun sign, I could clearly see indicators for low Vitamin D. Vitamin D support was needed. In astrology, as the Sun is primarily a fire sign, it does poorly when placed in water, air and earth signs. The Sun is also an indicator of your physical energy, vitality, creative force and self-esteem; it also rules the heart.

Vitamin D comes from the Sun and is a fire element. Health practitioners encourage you to get 20 minutes of Sun every day to maintain Vitamin D levels in your body. High Vitamin D levels in your body are vital in maintaining healthy functioning of all your body systems. This includes your immune, endocrine, cardiovascular, hormonal, skeletal and reproductive systems.

Under my Doctor's recommendation, I took high doses of Vitamin D for 6 weeks to bring my levels to above normal. Once done, I did a repeat blood test to confirm this.

Next, I looked at what was happening to the throat area, as the parathyroid is structurally situated on top of the thyroid gland in the neck. This is indicated by the second house in the chart, and any planets making challenging connections to the sign of Taurus.

I had planet Saturn which rules blockages, decay, restriction, and diminished blood flow travelling in my second house that rules the neck. Another indicator. As it was travelling in the sign of Sagittarius, I was lacking the mineral silica in the body. This was replaced with a course of tissue salts. I also replaced Vitamin K2 as this is ruled by planet Saturn.

Further investigation into this condition also revealed that the element Boron was needed for parathyroid health, so I replaced this also.

After 6 months of this strict routine, my parathyroid blood test reverted to normal. My symptoms disappeared and I have been experiencing increased vitality and clear thinking since. I still have my parathyroid blood test done every 3 months; my Doctor insists on it.

You may ask, that as an Astrologer, if I could see this coming in my chart why didn't I avoid it?

Most conditions usually start with psychological or emotional disharmony. This can relate back as far as childhood but in most cases, conditions start astrologically 2-3 years before the onset. My hyperparathyroidism actually started 3 years prior when I had adrenal fatigue. Planet Saturn crossed my ascendant. In Medical Astrology the ascendant is one of the most vital health points in the chart. Any planets affecting this point will bring disturbance to the physical body. My Doctors were concerned with my heart and fatigue issues at that time, so the parathyroid was overlooked.

Knowing an ailment is looming in the chart, you can increase certain vitamins, minerals and foods as they relate to the planets. It is often after you notice symptoms that you take action and formulate a plan. This is the nature of the human beast. Something has to go wrong before we choose to fix it.

As an Astrologer I have come to learn and understand that challenge motivates people towards betterment.

As you develop, you help others who face similar situations to grow. I believe we are here as a spirit that chooses to have physical experiences, to grow into the best version of ourselves, and to help others along the way.

Avoiding a lesson can be to your detriment and ultimately damage your health. Being aware of what you need to learn, developing the skills and integrating the lesson into your life, is far more beneficial than putting your head in the sand. This takes faith, courage, and awareness.

My philosophy of health and healing is as follows:

The element of Air captures the essence of what this book is about. It represents creativity, intelligence, adaptability, information, flow of energies and innate wisdom. The acronym A.I.R. defines this.

A   AWARENESS

Astrology and Ayurveda are the tools I use to cultivate awareness in two areas. First, the spiritual, in identifying life patterns, enabling people to learn their life lessons. Secondly, the medical, in bringing forth the psychosomatic causes underlying disease and imbalance in the body.

I   INFORMATION

This book provides education and information tailored to the individual. "Be Aware and Be Informed" is the mantra derived from the belief that people need to be educated in alternatives available to them, so they can choose the best options for their individual needs.

R   RESPONSIBILITY

The tools offered throughout this book aim to bring balance to your life, so you are better equipped to face life's challenges. As an evolved soul, it is your responsibility to become conscious by making correct choices that serve you and bring about your own ability to self-heal. The practitioner is only as useful as the client's willingness to take self-responsibility and make change for their own benefit.

My passion is to identify and decipher physical, emotional, psychological, and spiritual challenges that contribute to disease. By using Astrology, my mission is to be of service, to help identify areas of potential health challenges, and to encourage, support and clarify possible solutions.

Please Note: All names used in the case studies of this book are fictitious to protect my clients' privacy.

How to use this book

Before you rush to your Sun sign read here first.

The word horoscope is from the Greek word horoskopos with hora meaning "hour" + skopos meaning "watching".

In Medical Astrology, three planets: The Sun, Moon, Saturn, and the ascendant, will identify most medical ailments for a person. The ascendant is formed at the time of birth of the person. If you do not have a time of birth, this does not prevent you from having a workable chart. You can obtain a birth time from your family, birth certificate, hospital records or via muscle testing.

The date, time and place in the world in which you are born determines your Astrology chart which is a reflection (blueprint) of who you are, and in all areas of your life.

The Astrology chart is the map and you are the navigator.

The date you are born determines your Sun Sign e.g. if your birthdate is 11.11.1960, you are a Scorpio. The date of birth is vital when looking at health. As important as this is, you need to understand you are more than your Sun Sign. The Sun represents 1/10 of your total being. There are 10 planets that impact your life and life choices, not just 1 planet or sign.

Just as a car engine needs all its interconnected components to be well-maintained for the car to function efficiently, the same applies to Astrology. For you to function in a healthy manner you need to understand that you are part of a holistic connection which serves your entire being. This applies when looking at your chart for health issues and how to maintain your health.

In Astrology your health is determined by your whole chart.

Your personal life story manifests in relation to the connection the planets have with each other. This should be assessed and interpreted by a professional Medical Astrologer.

To simplify the matter, if you know your chart and know your Sun, Moon and Ascendant then just go to the sections that relate to those signs and read the information. Include as much information that you feel is appropriate for you and add these recommendations to your daily routines for optimal wellness and vitality.

Although you are your chart when it comes to a health assessment, The Sun, Moon and Ascendant can show your major body challenges if badly aspected (connected).

First you need a birth chart. For this you need your date, time and city of birth. If you do not have a chart go to www.astro.com, or email me on crscorpio1111@gmail.com submit these details and I will email a free chart to you. Print your chart out and put it aside for the moment. We all know the day we were born which relates to your Sun Sign. If all you do is just use the Sun Sign information this will strengthen your body constitution and increase your vitality, so this is an excellent start.

Secondly, you need to understand the astrological signs, as this is how they will appear on your chart. They are listed on the following page.

The Signs of the Zodiac

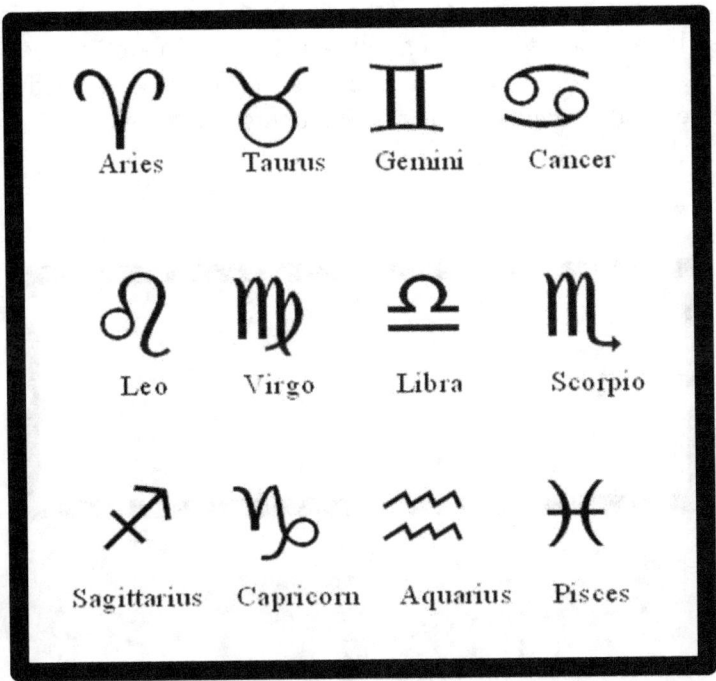

The next step is to identify the following in your chart:

Ascendant: this is the most critical point on your chart. This is determined by the *time* you were born. Your ascendant describes your typical characteristics and disposition. It also rules your first house in your chart that defines your physical body and any potential illness relating to it.

Sun: this is represented by your *date* of birth e.g. 11th November makes you a Scorpio. Your Sun sign determines your physical vitality and health. Also, the Sun reveals how you shine in the world and signifies father and male authority figures in your life.

Moon: this represents your soul memory, emotional nature and your bodily fluids. The Moon also signifies your mother or mother figure in your life.

Saturn: this is the karmic lord of the chart and is also known as Father Time. He represents the lesson you need to learn to evolve to your full potential. Also, this is where obstacles or blockages need to be identified and strengthened in relation to life and to health.

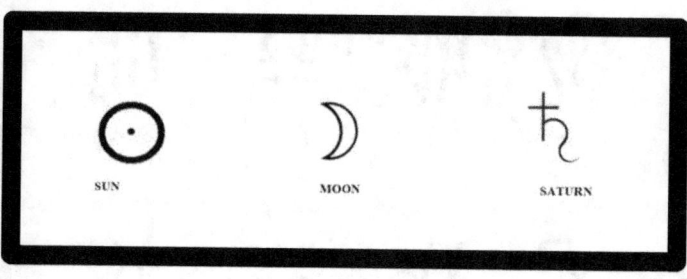

Practical example

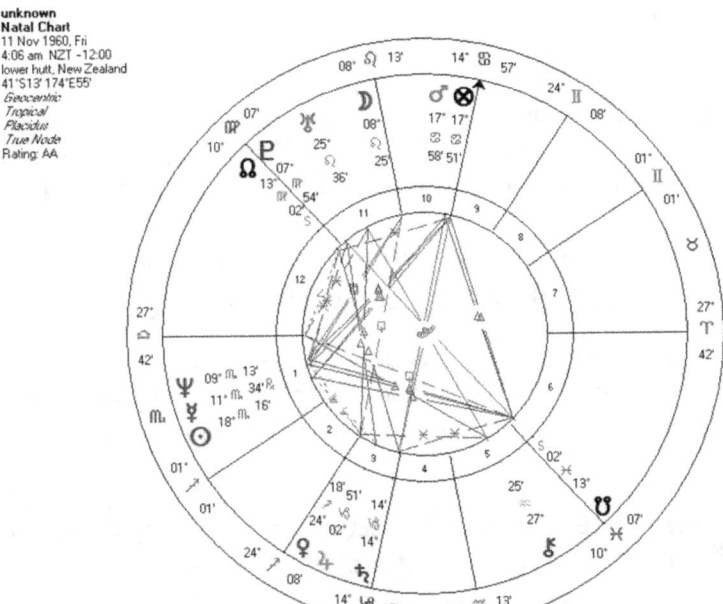

This is a typical astrology chart in the western system.

- First identify the Ascendant: LIBRA 27 degrees 42' and read the section relating to Libra
- Second identify the Sun: SCORPIO 18 degrees 16' and read the section relating to Scorpio
- Next identify the Moon: LEO 8 degrees 25' and read the section relating to Leo
- Last identify Saturn: CAPRICORN 14 degrees 14' and read the section relating to Capricorn. Planet Saturn shows potential blocks in your body, so read the *Associated Body Organs* and *Recommended Therapies* section only. Now read the sections on Leo, Libra, Scorpio and Capricorn (as relevant to the chart above).

As you read each section, you will notice not all the information will apply to you, and some of it will be spot on. You will recognise parts of yourself in what you read, and it will just feel right. We all have intuition which comes from our soul, and this cannot lie, always trust it. Take what applies to you only.

Naturally, the other planets and houses are involved in Astro-diagnosis, but for the purpose of this book and for non-astrologers we will keep it simple and just use Sun, Moon, Saturn and the Ascendant.

Now apply this formula to your own chart and use the *Personal Notes* page at the end of this chapter to write your findings.

With this information you can introduce practices into your daily life to strengthen your body. Continual bad habits and wrong choices will cause imbalance in the body which, if unattended, will eventually lead to disease.

Daily healthy choices maintain correct psychological, spiritual and emotional functioning which promotes physical wellness.

My approach to integrated health is to understand the physical, emotional and spiritual aspects of yourself to promote optimum wellness. <u>Live in Full Energy.</u>

Aries

March 21st to April 19th

Sign Profile

Aries is an action orientated fire sign. Aries people are known for their energy, drive, passion, inspiration, courage, impulsiveness, impatience, independence, adventurous spirit, and competitive nature.

Those born under Aries usually have a strong body constitution. They hate getting sick because it means they need to STOP. Aries is ruled by planet Mars and they love being constantly on the go. Due to their impatience, Aries often tend to be accident prone. They need to think before they act. It is not uncommon for an Aries to spike with high temperatures and sweat when unwell. This is how their body deals with disease. Even though they hate being sick, once they stop and allow themselves to rest, they tend to recover quickly.

Aries can 'burn the candle at both ends' believing they are invincible. Consequently, Aries will often suffer from adrenal exhaustion. Feelings of frustration and anger increase their cortisol levels which keeps their body in a constant state of inflammation. Heat produces dryness in the body which drains their adrenals causing fatigue. Learning how to manage their anger, eating meat in moderation, adding adrenal herbs into their daily routine, drinking copious amounts of cold water, physical exercise and breath work will benefit their body and their health. Food is fuel for the body and Aries tends to burn up fuel very quickly. A good breakfast and eating every few hours during the day is recommended especially if their job has a lot of physical activity.

Case Study

Andrew came to see me with complaints of feeling tired, having muscle pain, constipation, and headaches. Andrew was a courier and he was constantly on the move. He ate when he felt hungry, drank only about 1200mls of water a day, had a few beers to unwind after work, went to bed around 11pm, and loved his coffee.

On physical examination I could see his lips and skin were dry indicating dehydration. He had a white fluffy tongue and was fidgety when seated. He also stated he felt tired on waking, as if he hadn't slept at all.

I explained to him that a lack of water was adding to his headaches, dryness, constipation, and restlessness and so was the excess coffee drinking. After some discussion I recommended the following:

- Increase water to 2500mls daily
- Limit of one beer after work
- Take portable foods to work which include 3-4 pieces of fruit
- Retire by 10pm to gain full benefit of the sleep cycle
- Reduce inflammation in the body by having alkaline diet and meat limited to 3-4 servings a week
- If possible, go swimming - either before or after work
- Have a vitamin B12 and iron blood check
- No coffee or chocolate, drink tea or decaf coffee instead
- Take magnesium at night (helps with sleep and muscle pain)
- Have eyes tested (problem with his eyes may contribute to headaches)
- Tongue scrape every morning
- Increase spinach and vegetables with main meal
- Add psyllium husks to his diet
- Gave him a full regime on how to correct his digestion
- Gave him a breathing technique to use when stressed
- Recommend he add some herbs to support his adrenal system

I asked him to stay on this for 8 weeks. He emailed me and stated he was feeling much better. His blood test showed Vitamin B12 level was low and this was replenished. He was swimming most mornings and still following the plan I made for him and was sleeping more soundly, waking up feeling refreshed and full of energy.

Associated Body Organs

- Muscular and Adrenal systems.
- Body parts affected include brain, skull, head, face, eyes, ears, sinus, adrenal gland, pituitary gland, and blood.

Other body systems that need support to promote vitality for Aries sign are, the Skeletal, Endocrine, Urinary and the Lower Digestive system.

Aries people know when they are unbalanced because:

Aries people tend to become impatient and impulsive wanting everything now. They can be inconsiderate of others, thoughtless, self-centred, stubborn and do not take responsibility for their actions or in some cases non-action. When frustrated with themselves or with life, they can get angry quickly and will get over their anger just as quickly. Aries are prone to being more reactive than reflective. Once they cool down, they then tend to think more clearly.

How to overcome Stress

<u>Minimising Stress</u>
Aries are independent and competitive by nature. They do better in solitary sports unless they are the team captain.
They have a Pitta (heating) constitution, so any activities that include water are particularly beneficial. Aries have an abundance of energy to channel and they do well with short duration physical activities. If engaged with sports this will help manage their anger. As Aries love personal attention, they do well with personal trainers. Aries do well to channel excess energy into sports, preferably in the morning: short distance running, defensive martial arts, competitive sports, team sports, boxing, javelin, swimming, the gym, tennis, water sports and other adventurous activities.

Gentle walking, Tai Chi, mindfulness, or meditation can be very good at grounding the Martian energy.

Aries should avoid wearing the colour red when stressed, drinking alcohol, coffee and other caffeine-based beverages, and eating spicy foods that stimulate. They should wear blues and greens to promote calmness, drink plenty of water to keep cool and well hydrated, maintain a regular daily routine and eat every few hours as they burn up energy very fast. They should be actively focused when achieving their goals.

Recommended Therapies

Aromatherapy

Signature Oil – Rosemary
Rosemary is warming and stimulating in nature. Particularly good for the head and brain, it is excellent in treating headaches, sinusitis, and catarrh. Also used for refreshing a tired mind and improves memory.

Ayurveda

Dosha Constitution - Pitta the fire element. Primarily rules the head, brain, sinus, fevers, headaches, stroke, eyes and back of head to skull, blood, adrenal glands and muscular system.

Bach Flowers

Aries - Impatiens
Aries has a desire to lead, to be spontaneous and has trouble with structure. Impatiens will help with being less anxious, frustrated, and irritable that can lead to fear. Helps slow down the 'speedy' process in the mind. This enables any ideas or thoughts to be put into productive positive action.

Chakra

<u>Spiritual Chakra - Manipura</u>
Aries is ruled by Mars the God of War. It is quite natural for Arian types to be concerned with issues of power related to their own sense of self. This third chakra located at the solar plexus is connected to ego, personal power, autonomy, physical energy, metabolism, drive, courage, and personal will. This gives a strong sense of self-esteem and self-respect when in balance.

Signs of imbalance include ulcers, allergies, digestive disorders, liver and gallbladder ailments, low vitality, misplaced anger, and control issues, sensitivity to criticism, low self-esteem, introversion, and shame.

Colour

<u>BRIGHT RED</u> - the colour of action and passion

Positive - assertive, passion, alert, dynamic, warm and strong
Negative - angry, exhausted, weak-willed, impractical and cold

Balance negative vibrations by using blues, greens and browns.

Affirmation - 'Every day in every way I feel energised, assertive and alive.'

Crystals

<u>Bloodstone</u> - encourages caution, courage, renewal, healing, harmony, adaptability, strength, and helps to demonstrate unselfishness. It also supports the decision-making process and is good for meditation.
It physically supports immune, blood, lymphatic, metabolic, urinary and the spleen.

Herbs

- Ashwagandha, Holy basil, Astragalus or Rhodiola to support adrenal function
- Brahmi, Rosemary and Ginkgo to help improve memory
- Burdock and Gentian are helpful in purifying the blood
- Gotu Kola is beneficial for soothing nerves
- Honeysuckle is good for nervous headache, neuralgia, and itch
- Horseradish and garlic for sinus
- Nettles to promote blood flow
- Oats, Skullcap, Passionflower and Valerian to aid in soothing the Central Nervous System.

It is highly recommended that you consult a Naturopath or Herbalist if you choose to use herbs. Some herbs may be contraindicated with prescribed medicines. The safest way to use fresh herbs is as a brewed tea or in cooking.

Minerals

Aries are energetic, inspirational, visionary, dynamic, aggressive, impatient, enthusiastic, adventurous, hot-tempered, extroverted, and excitable. Prone to headaches, hypertension, eye disorders, fever, insomnia, cuts, burns, adrenal exhaustion and dental issues.

Essential minerals - chloride, calcium, iron, copper, selenium, sodium, phosphorus.

Enriched food sources - salt, dairy, sardines, green leafy vegetables, lean meat, shellfish, seafood, mushrooms, nuts seeds, lentils, avocados, yeast extract, poultry and whole grain.

Nutrition

Aries rules the face, head, adrenal glands, and the blood. With the Sun or other planets in Aries, prominent imbalances include: headaches, fevers, high stress levels, blood congestion, acidosis due to high meat consumption, high blood pressure, exhaustion, insomnia, ailments in connection to the ears, eyes and nose, hair loss, and accidents to the head in general.

Some helpful foods - whole grains, green leafy veggies, brewer's yeast, nuts, mushrooms, fish, dates, parsley, dried apricots, blackstrap molasses, strawberries, tomatoes, celery, cucumbers, lettuce and asparagus. Spicy, heating foods and stimulants should be avoided - they may cause over-stimulation of the nervous system.

Tissue Salt

Potassium Phosphate is also known as Kali Phos.

When lacking in potassium phosphate, Aries will exhibit anxiety, mental fatigue, lack of drive, insomnia, headache, alopecia (stress related), skin conditions, chronic fatigue, malaise, lethargy, photophobia and dilated pupils.

Foods containing potassium phosphate include: lettuce, cauliflower, cucumber, spinach, olives, radish, cabbage, onion, pumpkin, lentils, apples, potato, lima beans, walnuts and horseradish.

Vitamins

Foods containing essential vitamins suitable for Aries:

<u>A:</u>   Liver, carrots, parsley, sweet potato, spinach, mangoes, chives, tomatoes, and broccoli.

<u>B12:</u>   Liver, beef, chicken, oysters, scallops, fish, and cottage cheese.

<u>C:</u>   Citrus fruits, red chilli peppers, kale, parsley, cauliflower, broccoli, turnip greens, spinach, cabbage, mangoes, oysters, lima beans, strawberries, and raspberries.

<u>D:</u>   Fish liver oils, tuna, salmon, sardines and dairy.

<u>Folic Acid:</u>   Chicken and beef livers, asparagus, lettuce, broccoli, fresh orange juice, legumes, and dark leafy green vegetables.

> ### Recommended Daily Health Tip
> As an active fire sign, you are prone to dehydration. Stay well hydrated. Drink 3-4 litres of cold water daily. This will keep headaches at bay and help manage your fiery disposition.

Best Day and Number

Aries is ruled by Mars and is governed by Tuesday and the number 9.

Mantra

I exercise daily to keep myself grounded and focused.

Personal Notes:

Taurus

April 20th to May 20th

Sign Profile

Taurus is gentle natured, security conscious, dependable, sensual, grounded, steady, stubborn, possessive, and determined with a sensitive spirit.

The constitution of a Taurus is robust and sturdy. Taurus people have the ability to resist illness and will usually become unwell through overindulgence in rich and starchy foods. Being ruled by the planet Venus their love of carbohydrates and fine wine will often cause weight gain which contributes to many of their health conditions.

When it comes to their own self-care, the pleasure principle takes over. If it 'feels good' they will follow the path of least resistance. Ultimately, this is their downfall. Taurus will often choose to ignore any symptoms that start to manifest in their body. They believe their symptoms will either dissipate or that they are not sick and will 'tough it out'. By the time they finally go to their doctor, the symptoms have taken root and turned into a chronic illness. By this stage, time and a major change in their lifestyle is imperative in order for them to become well again.

When I see a client who has major planets in Taurus or is born in the sign of Taurus, I always ask them to get their thyroid and parathyroid checked via a blood test. The thyroid has a major role to play with this sign. When unbalanced it can contribute to weight gain or weight loss, sluggish energy, brain fog and emotional imbalance.

The neck and shoulders are the areas of the body where Taurus will hold their stress. This can result in frozen shoulder which can be a precursor to type 2 diabetes. Deep tissue massage and daily neck exercises work well in releasing stress in this area.

Case Study

Tina came to see me with symptoms of low energy, weight gain, brain fog, napping in the afternoon around 3-4pm, depression, a broken tooth and body aches and pains, especially in the joints. She had her haemoglobin tested which was normal and her thyroid tests were also normal. Her Astrological Chart indicated problems in the thyroid area, as well as a lack of vitamin D. I recommended the following:

- 20-minute walk in sunlight daily
- Get a parathyroid, vitamin D and calcium blood test (her results came back very low Vitamin D level, calcium level was normal and parathyroid level was high). Due to these results Tina was diagnosed with secondary hyperparathyroidism
- Vitamin D replacement was needed
- 5HTP with magnesium to be taken at night
- Brahimi tea or herbs for the brain
- Add the herb rosemary to meals for the brain
- Add iodine to her diet via fish, seaweed or salt
- Add boron and silica to support the parathyroid
- Take Vitamin K2 daily

Due to her condition she started having regular blood tests every 3 months. Once the Vitamin D was replenished and was at a healthy level Tina felt more energetic, stopped napping in the afternoon and was more motivated with her daily activities.

A parathyroidectomy was an option for her, but Tina decided to stay on the natural path with close monitoring by her doctor. That was 4 years ago. Tina has not needed a surgical procedure. She is following my guidelines and also has annual Vitamin D checks.

<u>Special Note for thyroid and parathyroid conditions</u>

Recommended that you have regular thyroid, parathyroid and vitamin D tests done (they are 3 separate blood tests) to make sure they are within limits. A low thyroid level can manifest as low energy and weight gain. Make sure your diet is high in iodine.

Nutrition

There are foods that interfere with the uptake of iodine and thyroid function that need to be avoided. They include:

Cabbage, broccoli, turnips, mustard, spinach, peaches, sweet potato, brussels sprouts, strawberries, kale, cauliflower, pears, millet, gluten, tempeh, bamboo shoots, canola oil, horseradish, bok choy, maize, soybeans, and related products

You need good iodine, selenium, and zinc levels to keep your thyroid healthy.

Associated Body Organs

- Metabolic system
- Hormonal system
- Body parts affected: neck, tonsils, throat, pharynx, vocal cords, thyroid glands, shoulders, cervical vertebra, lower jaw, base of brain, kidneys, and muscles in the shoulders.

Other body systems that need support to promote vitality for Taurus sign are, the Circulatory, Reproductive, Elimination, and the Cardiac system.

Taurus knows when they are unbalanced because:

Taurus can become bull-headed and will not listen to anyone. Being rigid in their decisions can keep them stuck in a rut. When this happens, they lack motivation, become introverted, can be resentful and are prone to laziness. When in this state they will indulge in pleasure foods for comfort and security. An unbalanced Taurus will exhibit signs of being possessive and dependent. Taurus does not like change. As a consequence, there is a need to control all aspects of their lives which only bring them disharmony and contributes to illness.

How to overcome Stress

Minimising Stress

For Taurus, regular exercise is required to maintain weight. Once motivated, they have the endurance to go long distances as they understand how to pace their energy and breath. Wearing yellow and orange will stimulate activity when they feel stuck or unmotivated. Adding hot spices to diet will promote metabolism and therefore aid digestion. Taurus loves to wind down after work, playing peaceful music in a serene environment will satisfy their soul. Taurus will probably have a golden voice so singing to their heart's content will not only soothe their soul but will also strengthen their immunity. As they are very tactile, sacred stone massage therapy and head and shoulder oil massage, also known as Shirodhara, will make them feel good and centred. Both are Ayurvedic Therapies.

Often Taurus people have sturdy builds and are usually very strong. They love good food so a tendency of being overweight will bring health issues which is why daily exercise is important.

Recommended exercise includes judo, wrestling, weightlifting, ballroom dancing, rock and roll dancing, long distance marathons, judo, picking fruit and cardio workout.

Recommended Therapies

Aromatherapy

Signature Oil - Rose
Rose is known as the "Queen of oils" and is an aphrodisiac, stimulating, an antidepressant and carminative by nature. Specifically benefits the heart and chest area, improving your sense of value, love, self-worth and inner security.

Ayurveda

<u>Dosha Constitution</u> - Kapha the water element. Primarily rules the face, shoulders, cervical vertebra, neck, larynx, vocal cords, thyroid, shoulders, cerebellum, and metabolic system.

Bach Flowers

<u>Taurus - Gentian</u>
Will help Taurus overcome self-doubt and lack of faith. Taurus may become easily discouraged and create negative thoughts leading to depression. Gentian adds more sweetness to life and helps to counteract negative emotions. By balancing their moods, they can then become more motivated.

Chakra

<u>Spiritual Chakra - Anahata</u>
Venus rules the heart, this fourth chakra, and is about the relationship they have with themself, their sense of personal values, self-acceptance, and self-compassion. Once achieved, you can then extend real love to others.

Signs of imbalance: heart related diseases, high blood pressure, mistrust, grief, holding onto past hurts, melancholy and being unable to give and receive freely.

Colour

<u>PINK</u> - the colour of love and affection

Positive - calming, soothing, increases confidence, affectionate, harmonious and loving.
Negative - smothering, sickly, overwhelmed and stagnant.

Balance negative vibrations by using more orange, yellows, reds and burgundy.

Affirmation - 'I am full of love for myself and others.'

Crystals

Rose Quartz - promotes clarity, balances and heals emotion, reinstates self-love, promotes receptivity to the arts and balances yin-yang energy. Opens the heart which aids in dissolving stress and tension. Clears anger, cools temper and alleviates guilt. Physically will help to overcome trauma, addiction, heart problems, will aid in fertility, support lungs, kidneys, and the adrenals.

Herbs

- Bearberry (Uva Ursi) good for chronic throat infections
- Coltsfoot excellent for hoarseness, colds, and coughs
- Gymnema blocks the intestinal absorption of sugar and regulates blood sugar levels
- Slippery elm, Kelp, and Fenugreek support the thyroid gland
- Sage for sore throats and to strengthen the nervous system
- Trikatu - an Ayurvedic herb that stimulates metabolism

It is highly recommended that you consult a Naturopath or Herbalist if you choose to use herbs. Some herbs may be contraindicated with prescribed medicines. The safest way to use fresh herbs is as a brewed tea or added in cooking.

Minerals

Taurus is dependable, practical, solid, loyal, stubborn, introverted, and rigid. They find it difficult to make change and when it comes to their own health, they only seek help when absolutely necessary. They should sing to strengthen their thyroid gland. Prone to tonsillitis, laryngitis, thyroid, kidney stones, obesity, prostate enlargement, neck strain and hormonal imbalance.

Essential minerals - iodine, chromium, copper

Enriched food sources - iodised salt, seaweed, seafood, shellfish, red meat, liver, cheese, whole grain cereal, mushrooms, nuts, seeds, and cocoa.

Nutrition

Taurus rules the metabolic system, thyroid, tonsils, neck, throat, lower jaw and vocal cords, trapezium, mastoid, oesophagus, occipital area, neck, and shoulders. Common ailments include: thyroid malfunction, sore throat, excess storage, glandular fever, laryngitis, polyps, stiff neck and shoulders, holding onto emotions, indulgences.

Beneficial foods include: seaweed, green leafy veggies, seafood, spinach, cabbage, peaches, beans, potatoes, blackberries, pomegranate, strawberries, spirulina, and chlorella. Soy products also help thyroid regulation; drink at least 2 litres of water daily. Excess sugar, starch and dairy should be avoided. Care needs to be taken not to indulge in food in place of emotional satiety, especially rich foods that cause weight gain.

Tissue Salt

Sodium Sulphate is also known as Nat Phos.

When lacking in sodium sulphate Taurus will exhibit fluid retention, watery stool, weepy eczema, physical and emotional congestion, asthma, bronchitis, nausea, liver congestion and jaundice.

Foods containing sodium sulphate include beetroot, spinach, horseradish, cauliflower, onion, pumpkin, cucumber and swiss chard.

Vitamins

Foods containing essential vitamins suitable for Taurus:

B6: Lean meat, poultry, fish, eggs, whole-wheat breads and cereals, nuts, bananas, soybeans, brown rice, lentils, lima beans, avocados, spinach, potatoes, cauliflower, popcorn, and leeks.

E: Vegetable oil, wheat germ, soybeans, whole grains, raw nuts, raw seeds and eggs.

Niacin: Lean meat, pulses, poultry, potatoes, salmon, tuna, peanuts, liver, beef, veal, mushrooms, brown rice, and dried peaches.

> **Recommended Daily Health Tip**
> Add iodised or sea salt to your meals. The iodine will help maintain thyroid health.

Best Day and Number
Taurus is ruled by Venus and is governed by Friday and the number 6.

Mantra

I enjoy good quality food that is healthy for me.

Personal Notes:

Gemini

May 21st to June 20th

Sign Profile

Gemini is known for being versatile, social, fun loving, inquisitive, intelligent, nervous, informative, superficial, with a quick and changeable nature.

Gemini people's constitution is variable due to their unpredictable nature. Being ruled by planet Mercury, they have a thirst for knowledge which over stimulates their nervous and mental systems.

Geminis have quick intelligence and body metabolism. They tend to eat on the run, not giving their body what it needs to function well. Consequently, their body and mind are often in a constant hypervigilant state. This state depletes essential nutrients often leading to body breakdown.

Gemini has rulership over the chest area and Asthma is a condition they may suffer from. In Ayurveda, Asthma is connected to problems with the colon. Incomplete evacuation, constipation, diarrhoea or offensive flatus are all indicators that may contribute to asthma. Correcting digestion, practising deep breathing, sleeping with the window open at night, swimming, allergy testing and being smoke free will help minimise this condition.

Case Study

Gerald came to see me with symptoms of anxiety, being unfocused, having self-doubt, restlessness, and irritability. His Astrology chart showed a Stellium (more than 3 planets in one sign) in Gemini which was intensified by planet Uranus. He also had no earth in his chart.

Gerald's diet was not great. He ate on the run, often from the local takeaway and he loved to drink Coca Cola or a Red Bull as they 'kept him going'. For a snack it was usually coffee and cake around 3pm.

It was clear to me that his lifestyle was aggravating his nervous system, which affected his cognitive abilities and mood. After a long discussion around how sugar and coffee affected his body, I recommended the following;

- Start the day with muesli and fruit
- One cup of coffee daily preferably before noon
- Replace sugar with stevia
- Carry portable foods like protein bars and nuts
- Drink bottled water with a couple of drops of stevia for taste instead of Coca Cola
- Include spinach, broccoli, whole grains, legumes, almonds, brown rice, eggs, potatoes, avocados, and bananas – daily
- Take magnesium supplement morning and night
- Have an oil massage weekly
- Practice breathing exercises daily
- Do Yoga, Tai Chi or Qigong and swimming
- Good fish oils, omega 3, flaxseed oils added to smoothies and salads
- Take Vitamin B with folate and zinc daily
- Lemon balm tea which is good for anxiety
- Lavender, sweet marjoram and bitter orange are calming for the nerves
- Ashwagandha can be taken for nerve support
- Walk barefoot on grass whenever you can

After one month, Gerald reported he was feeling much better, more focused and less irritable. He had taken up Yoga and I advised him to reduce his oil massages to monthly.

Associated Body Organs

- Central Nervous System
- Respiratory system
- Body parts affected include lungs, trachea, bronchi, diaphragm, fingers, hands, arms,
- shoulders, collar bone, thymus, nerves, thoracic spine and bones of the thoracic region
- Oxygenation of the blood is also under this influence.

Other body systems that need support to promote vitality for Gemini sign are the Immune system, Lymphatic system, Autonomic Nervous system, and the Upper Digestive system.

Geminis know when they are unbalanced because:

Geminis can become scattered, ungrounded, and unfocused. When Geminis are in this state, they cannot complete their many tasks and are unable to make clear decisions. Their minds are overstimulated, and they are restless. As a sign, Gemini is more in their mind than in their body, and when unstable they can be superficial, cynical, and undecided. They will often give one face of themselves to others while keeping the other hidden. Hence the reason they can be known as 'two-faced'.

How to best overcome Stress

<u>Minimising Stress</u>
Geminis need plenty of fresh air to soothe their highly active nervous systems. Geminis are versatile, quick and need to include a variety of different exercises to be happy as they get bored with repetition. It is not uncommon for them to part-take in more than one sport as they can manage many things at the same time. Geminis are usually well coordinated as they instinctively know how to connect their mind to their body.

Activities that suit their constitution on a regular basis include ice skating, tennis, badminton, dancing, gymnastics, sprinting, skiing, Yoga, meditation, swimming, Zumba, fencing, golf, and Tai Chi.

As mentioned above, eating root vegetables daily will keep them grounded. Wearing greens and earth colours will calm their nerves and keep them focused. They need intellectual stimulation so should keep a daily journal; matching their wits against others in board games and card games suits them. Debates are also good for them – so, start up a debate team. Regular oil massage and Shirodhara therapy (an Ayurvedic therapy), helps keep Gemini balanced.

Recommended Therapies

Aromatherapy

Signature Oil - Basil
Basil is a mentally stimulating, antispasmodic, cephalic (clears congestion in the head), antibacterial oil which suits the Gemini constitution well. It helps bring harmony to the mind and calms the nerves.

Ayurveda

Dosha Constitution - Vata the air element. Primarily rules the shoulders, upper arms, chest, lungs, hands, blood oxygenation and central nervous system.

Bach Flowers

Gemini - Cerato
This will help Geminis with their confidence, prevent them scattering their thoughts and energy, and will aid in focusing their curiosity which will help with calming the nervous system. Will assist in communicating more effectively, being more social and interactive with others.

Chakra

Spiritual Chakra - Vishuddha
Mercury rules the throat chakra, the fifth chakra, and Geminis love to socialise and like to be known for the knowledge they gather. This chakra governs communication, speaking and honouring your truth, choice and freewill.

Signs of imbalance include speech impediments, sore throat, cough, neck problems, laryngitis, thyroid imbalance, respiratory and/or hearing problems and lies.

Colour

GREEN - the colour of healing and balance

Positive - harmonious, balanced, sharing, protective and secure
Negative - insincere, selfish, jealous, threatened, and insecure

Balance negative vibrations by using more brown, purple, and white.

Affirmation - 'I am balanced, centred and secure in my emotions'

Crystals

Chrysocolla - gives strength with balance in expression and communication, dissipates nervous tension, helps Geminis to become attuned with mother earth and aids in understanding of others. Helps to clear the aura by drawing out negative emotions.

Physically supports cellular structure, respiratory, circulatory, digestive, urinary, infections of throat, tonsils, menstrual cramps, and pre-menstrual syndrome.

Herbs

- Ashwagandha and Brahmi to soothe the nervous system
- Elecampane for protection of the lungs
- Garlic and Echinacea to aid in improving the immune system
- Lavender helpful in calming nerves and anxiety
- Lily of the Valley helpful with nervous disorders
- Skullcap to strengthen and relax the nervous system

It is highly recommended that you consult a Naturopath or Herbalist if you choose to use herbs. Some herbs may be contraindicated with prescribed medicines. The safest way to use fresh herbs is as a brewed tea or in cooking.

Minerals

Geminis are social, active, lively, nervous, highly strung, mentally active, communicative, and witty. They tend to overwork their nervous system and need adequate sleep to replenish. Easily distracted, they need to learn to be still and focus. Prone to asthma, bronchitis, nervous disorders, stiff shoulders, and carpel tunnel syndrome.

Essential minerals - magnesium, calcium, potassium, sodium

Enriched food sources - dairy, salt, canned anchovies, pulses, nuts, whole grain cereals, dried fruits, green vegetables, sardines, green leafy vegetables, avocados, fresh fruit and potatoes.

Nutrition

Gemini rules the respiratory system including lungs, diaphragm and thoracic cavity, collarbones, oxygenation of blood, the trachea, arms, hands, fingers, the tubes of the body, and central nervous system. Gemini people commonly suffer from: nervous disorders, bronchitis, shallow breathing, asthma, fractures of collarbones, arms, and hands.

Beneficial foods: root veggies, cheese, broccoli, cauliflower, corn, apricots, peaches, nuts, seeds, eggs, lecithin, and essential fatty acids, green leafy veggies, liquid chlorophyll, chamomile tea, broccoli, almonds, prunes, wheat germ, figs, watercress, tahini and parsley.

Tissue Salt

Potassium Chloride is also known as Kali Mur.

When lacking in potassium chloride Geminis may exhibit dandruff, herpetic ulcers, congested lymphatics, white phlegm, glandular problems, inflammations, middle ear and blood clotting problems.

Foods containing potassium chloride include green beans, carrots, asparagus, sprouts, beets, cauliflower, tomato, sweet corn, spinach, celery, oranges, pears, pineapple, peaches, plums, and apricots.

Vitamins

Foods containing essential vitamins suitable for Gemini:

B1: Pork, liver, heart, kidneys, fish, potatoes, nuts, pulses, rice bran, soy milk, rolled oats, lima beans, peas, lentils, and mung beans.

B12: Liver, beef, chicken, oysters, scallops, fish, and cottage cheese.

C: Citrus fruits, red chilli peppers, kale, parsley, cauliflower, broccoli, turnip greens, sprouts, spinach, cabbage, mangoes, oysters, lima beans, strawberries, and raspberries.

D: Fish liver oils, tuna, salmon, sardines and dairy.

> ### Recommended Daily Health Tip
> Have Omega 3 in your daily diet. Omega 3 keeps the nervous system nourished and protected so you do not feel so scattered.

Best Day and Number

Gemini is ruled by Mercury and is governed by Wednesday and the number 5.

Mantra

I love my good oils and so does my Nervous System.

Personal Notes:

Cancer

June 21st to July 22nd

Sign Profile

The sign of Cancer is known for being nurturing, protective, receptive, sentimental, intuitive, creative, clingy, moody, kind, caring and gentle by nature.

Cancers' constitution is fluid by nature as they tend to absorb whatever is happening in their environment. Their body is usually very curvaceous and can retain fluids and experience bloating especially if they are not doing regular exercise.

Cancer has a strong nurturing instinct and will express this freely to family and friends. This can become very smothering for some people and Cancer needs to give space to others and themselves so growth can occur.

Food and feeding others are a passion. Often when Cancer feels insecure or upset, they will turn to food as a source of comfort. Many will suffer with weight problems if this is a continuous habit.

Due to their deep sensitivities and being ruled by the Moon, Cancer is known for being moody. This is intensified when there is a full moon.

When Cancer takes on 'the world' and neglects themselves, stomach ulcers may result.

Avoid spicy foods, fermented foods, milk products, coffee, alcohol, smoking, raw fruit, vegetables, grains, and nuts; reduce stress, particularly worrying. Include warm drinks, soups, vitamins C, E and zinc, alkaline diet, Aloe Vera and Slippery Elm.

Case Study

Cathy came to me complaining of constipation, stomach pain, reflux and feeling sluggish due to feeling overweight. Her confidence was low, and she was very emotional. After an in-depth conversation with her I recommended the following:

- Avoid cold and raw foods
- Walk for 20 minutes twice a day
- Eat fresh, seasonal locally grown foods
- Boost digestion with ½ teaspoon grated ginger, ½ teaspoon lemon juice and a pinch of rock salt 15 minutes before meals
- Fast one day a week with fluids only, warm soups and herbal teas
- Start your day with warm water, juice of half a lemon and a pinch of ginger to promote digestion
- Ideally eat small meals 3-4 times daily
- Have your main meal in the middle of the day
- Have your light dinner as early as possible
- Eat when you are hungry
- Avoid white processed foods
- Eat food cooked with love
- Use digestive herbs and spices in your cooking (if necessary) e.g. ginger, cumin, garlic, cardamom, cinnamon, fennel, fenugreek, rosemary, peppermint, dill, aniseed, and caraway
- Chew all food thoroughly before swallowing
- Eat meat 1-2 times a week and it needs to be cooked well in the form of soups and casseroles for easy digestion
- When upset go for a walk
- Eat plenty of celery as this is a natural diuretic
- Have regular massage and lymphatic drainage
- Have Aloe Vera 20mls morning and night
- Work on resolving issues with your mother
- DO NOT WEIGH YOURSELF, monitor your energy levels and mood responses instead
- Wear more yellows and orange
- Purchase a rose quartz necklace and wear it
- Alkaline diet

Cathy came to see me several times as emotional support was vital to her progress. She kept to the plan the best she could, and her body weight did fluctuate. She did lose several kilos over time. More importantly she achieved self-acceptance which boosted her confidence regardless of her weight.

Associated Body Organs

- Lower Digestive System.
- Body parts affected include digestive system, stomach, breasts, sternum, pancreas, saliva, blood and plasma, gallbladder, uterus, vertebral discs, pericardium, and synovial joints.

Other body systems that need support to promote vitality for Cancer sign are, the Muscular, Adrenal, Skeletal, Endocrine and the Urinary system.

Cancer know when they are unbalanced because:

Cancer can be very moody and extremely sensitive especially around the monthly full moon. Their emotions can go to extremes and they may seek comfort food to feel better. Let's set the scene, a big carton of ice cream, dressed in pyjamas watching a chick flick and indulging themselves with self-pity. Normally house-proud, in this state they are untidy, unreliable and tend to hold a grudge with others. Can be self-sacrificial to the point where they no longer nurture themselves.

How best to overcome Stress

Minimising Stress

Cancer loves the water. A water environment will feed their creativity and intuition. Being involved in water sports like swimming, diving, sailing, surfing, and water polo really satisfies their soul.

Wearing colours of yellow and orange will promote self-esteem and self-expression. They need to surround themselves with positive people who **do not** need any mothering. This will help to develop a strong sense of personal identity.

As Cancer is strongly creative, an artistic outlet is a great tool to express their inner personality. They need to learn to channel some of the caring, nurturing energy that they give others and pamper themselves more. Invest in yourself and have weekly facials, massages, and spa treatments. Listen to soothing music while you work, this will really chill you out.

If Cancer is strong in your astrology chart, then you love the comforts of home. Getting out and exercising may be a mission. Ideally an exercise routine from home would be perfect. Involve the kids or a friend. If you have a pacer, someone to meet several times a week who encourages you, your results will be better. Recommended exercises are - having a gym at home, kicking the ball or chasing the kids in the park, walking or running the dog, exercising to music and exercise video workouts in your own home. Being involved in any kind of water sports will really nurture you.

Recommended Therapies

Aromatherapy

Signature Oil - Blue Chamomile
Blue Chamomile is the 'mothering oil'. It is calming, soothing, gentle, analgesic, sedative, antispasmodic and digestive. Works well with all ailments related to the stomach and is gentle enough to use on infants and children.

Ayurveda

Dosha Constitution - Kapha the water element. Primarily rules the chest, ribs, stomach, breasts, uterus, and the upper digestive system.

Bach Flowers

Cancer - Clematis
Prone to withdrawing into themselves and may have trouble 'being in reality'. This is due to often being in a dreamlike or fantasy state. They retreat into this state as a form of escapism as they are very emotional and sensitive. Clematis helps to deal with their emotions, it is grounding and helps connect them to their environment.

Chakra

<u>Spiritual Chakra - Ajna</u>
Known as the brow, this is the sixth chakra; its role is linking you to your sense of knowing or intuition, wisdom, emotional intelligence, psychic awareness, dreams, and visions. Cancers have a natural ability of knowing; they just need to learn to trust it. It also allows them to see the big picture clearly with a positive outlook.

Signs of imbalance include headaches, problems with the Central Nervous System, vision problems, hallucinations, and illusions.

Colour

<u>WHITE</u> - the colour of insight and receptiveness

Positive-cleanliness, innocence, purity, aura protection
Negative-clinical, cold, detachment, sterile, lifeless

Balance negative vibrations by using more yellow, orange, and blue

Affirmation- 'I surround my aura and body with the spiritual white light of protection.'

Crystals

<u>Moonstone</u> - improves intuition and receptivity and connects to the feminine. Aids in deep emotional healing. Useful for men to help access their emotional self.

Physically works well with hyperactive children, emotional stress, menstrual and PMS related disorders, digestive, reproductive, hormonal and the pineal systems. Helps to alleviate insomnia, fluid retention, and degenerative conditions, also good for skin, eyes, and hair.

Herbs

- Chamomile calms the nerves and is a mild digestive
- Honeysuckle good for stomach cramps
- Peppermint and spearmint to aid digestion
- Poke root is suitable for lumpy breasts
- Raspberry leaf aids in conception
- Slippery elm will soothe digestion if inflamed

It is highly recommended that you consult a Naturopath or Herbalist if you choose to use herbs. Some herbs may be contraindicated with prescribed medicines. The safest way to use fresh herbs is as a brewed tea or in cooking.

Minerals

Cancer people are emotional, moody, overprotective, nurturing, quiet, family orientated and kind. They tend to internalise their feelings which can lead to disease. They need to learn to nourish themselves as much as they nourish others. Prone to anaemia, constipation, depression, indigestion, gallstones, weight/fluid gain and breast trouble.

Essential minerals - potassium, chloride, phosphorus

Enriched food sources - avocados, fresh fruit, potatoes, nuts, salt, milk, cheese, poultry, fish, seafood, seeds and wholegrain.

Nutrition

Cancer rules all the fluid filled areas in the body including stomach, breasts, uterus, pericardium, gall bladder and glycogen storage in the liver. Other ruler ships include the sternum, sinus cavity, salivary glands, bone marrow and chest. Common ailments include: digestive ailments, coughs, mal-absorption, gallstones, gastric mucus, physical symptoms brought on by emotional imbalance, worry and nervousness, uterine disorders.

Beneficial foods include fresh fruit and veggies, goat's milk, cottage cheese, eggs, rye, fish, citrus fruit, papaya, peppermint, steamed or lightly cooked foods, bananas, apricots, figs, kidney beans, lentils, spinach, sweet potato, sardines, seeds, parsley, kelp and molasses. Avoid cakes and pastries, eating as a source of emotional nourishment, and eating when worried or anxious as digestion may become sluggish.

Tissue Salt

Calcium Fluoride is also known as Calc Fluor.

When lacking in calcium fluoride Cancer will be prone to sensitive teeth, the enamel on their teeth will be affected, weakness of bone, varicose veins, cracked tongue, prolapsed conditions, hard cysts and loss of elasticity and strength in connective tissue.

Foods containing calcium fluoride include milk, eggs, cabbage, pumpkin, watercress, and lettuce.

Vitamins

Foods containing essential vitamins suitable for Cancer:

A: Liver, carrots, parsley, sweet potato, spinach, mangoes, chives, tomatoes, and broccoli.

B2:   Milk, yoghurt, eggs, meat, poultry, fish, liver, almonds, mushrooms, millet, parsley, cashew nuts, lentils, avocados, rye, broccoli, mung beans, and asparagus.

C: Citrus fruits, red chilli peppers, kale, parsley, cauliflower, broccoli, turnip greens, sprouts, spinach, cabbage, mangoes, oysters, lima beans, strawberries, and raspberries.

> **Recommended Daily Health Tip**
> Add digestive enzymes and probiotics for healthy digestion.

Best Day and Number

Cancer is ruled by the Moon and is governed by Monday and the number 2.

Mantra

I nurture myself first so I can nurture others better.

Personal Notes:

Leo

July 23rd to August 22nd

Sign Profile

Leo, the King of the Jungle, is famous for being loyal, proud, confident, egotistical, creative, bossy, arrogant, generous, passionate, affectionate, and demanding.

Leo is very fortunate as a sign because the Sun, which rules vitality, is in rulership. This means they have a strong body constitution, unless afflicted, in their chart.

Leos are very generous and gregarious and love to entertain. Their love of fine dining will contribute to atherosclerosis (hardening of the arteries) which brings on heart attacks, common for this sign.

Ruled by the Sun, Leos are born to shine, to spread their joy and creativity to others directly from their heart. They are not great followers and prefer to be the boss in all-important aspects of their life. The sooner they get to their place of bliss the happier they will be.

Many Leos suffer with back pain. This is primarily because they love to be in control and do not delegate. The back is the support structure in life. Always stand up straight with shoulders back. Make sure to be sitting upright when seated. Always bend at the knees when lifting. Sleep on a well-supported firm mattress. Practise Yoga or core and back exercises daily. Oil massage helps to release tensions held in your back. Have a good chiropractor. Make sure you are not overweight as this adds stress to your knees and back. For pain, take an herbal anti-inflammatory and use heat packs if needed. Add magnesium to your health routine.

Case Study

Levi came to me with concerns about his heart health. He mentioned his father and grandfather both died from a heart attack and feared he would also experience the same fate. Heart disease tends to run in families and his astrology chart indicated the same. I applauded him on choosing to be proactive. After discussion around his diet, exercise routine and examination of his blood tests (which he brought with him) I recommended the following:

- Minimise stress as this increases heart rate
- Magnesium to be taken at night
- Eat at no later than 7pm; eating late can press on the heart causing discomfort
- Avoid sugar, starch, alcohol and smoking
- Include foods rich in potassium, magnesium vitamin E and vitamin C
- Rosehip tea can be taken freely
- CQ10 300mg at night as we lose this enzyme as we get older
- Regular cholesterol and blood pressure checks
- Garlic and vitamin C help reduce cholesterol
- Saffron in cooking supports heart function.
- Nose bleeds may indicate high blood pressure. Have this checked by your doctor
- Find your joy in life and shine
- Alkaline diet is best no butter or hard cheese
- Drink 2.5-3 litres of water daily
- Exercise 30 minutes twice a day, walking is best
- Maintain a healthy weight

I followed up with Levi two months later to see how he was progressing. He confirmed that his bad cholesterol (LDL) had reduced and his good cholesterol (HDL) had improved. He had lost 4 kilos and was happy with that. The most significant change for him was that he did not feel fear anymore. Partly because his blood results were better but importantly because he was taking preventative measures around his own health. This made him feel mentally and emotionally well. He also started drama classes which he loves.

Associated Body Organs

- Cardiac system and circulatory system.
- Body parts affected include heart, spleen, spinal column including its nerves and marrow, pancreas, thoracic spine, and blood.

Other body systems that need support to promote vitality for Leo sign are the Circulatory, Reproductive, Elimination and the Metabolic system.

Leos know when they are unbalanced because:

Leo can be very generous but when unsettled their generosity can turn into extravagance. Their personality in this state will be overbearing, bossy, arrogant, lazy, conceited, and proud. Leo loves to be in charge whatever the situation, but with a negative mind-set they are controlling, demanding, intolerant, unbending and patronising. They will usually lose their creative passion or have a distorted view of their creativity. The joy in their life is misplaced and they constantly seek approval from others.

How best to overcome Stress

Activities to Minimise Stress

Leos do well to be outdoors and exposed to plenty of sunshine. Like a typical lion you love to just lie in the sun and be plain lazy at times. This only becomes counterproductive when it becomes a habit. Leos love action and have a lot of energy to burn when they are not lying around. They are driven and focus on the outcome, so when focused attaining their goal is paramount. They love action. Regular exercise like running, riding, wrestling, Yoga, football, full body workouts, cardio circuits, dynamic dance, and weightlifting are good choices to include in their regular exercise routine.

Being very artistic, having an outlet for creative ideas calms the drama queen in them. Suitable outlets include photography, film, acting, music, painting, jewellery design, drama, and dance. They love socializing and sharing their good fortune and graces with close supportive friends and family. Having fun relaxes them and spending time with children connects them to their inner child. Be joyous.

Recommended Therapies

Aromatherapy

Signature Oil - Jasmine
Jasmine is the "King of oils". It is an aphrodisiac, antidepressant, and is cooling for Leo's fiery temperament. Jasmine oil brings balance, confidence and helps to move through darkness, into the sunshine.

Ayurveda

Dosha Constitution - Pitta the fire element. Primarily rules the thoracic vertebra, solar plexus, spleen, spinal cord, spine, heart, body vitality, blood, marrow, and cardiac system.

Bach Flowers

Leo - Vervain

This will help get passion back, be more tolerant of others and help you feel excited about life. At times Leo will feel other people's needs are more important than their own as they have a strong need to shine and be creative. Honouring their own needs and passion will develop self-love.

Chakra

Spiritual Chakra - Sahasrara
Positioned at the top of the head, the seventh chakra is known to connect you to your higher self, universal truth, expanded consciousness and spiritual wisdom. Ruled by the Sun this is the total integration point of yourself aligned with soul self.

Signs of imbalance include confusion, depression, obsessive behaviour, an inability to learn, issues with attachment, epilepsy, and dementia.

Colour

GOLD - the colour of abundance and vitality

Positive - happy, intelligent, logical, optimistic, forgiving and light

Negative - irrational, heavy, sad, nervous, vindictive, and disorderly

Balance negative vibrations by using more green, brown and orange

Affirmation- 'I am filled with light and happiness.'

Crystals

Sunstone - This is appropriate as it promotes self-worth, confidence, optimism, passion, enthusiasm, leadership and self-healing powers. Helps heal sore throats, reduces stomach tension, relieves ulcers, treats cartilage and spinal problems.

Herbs

- Digitalis which strengthens the heart muscle
- Dill, fennel, mint, parsley, saffron and chamomile as teas or added to diet
- Hawthorne is a strong antioxidant for the heart
- Mistletoe is a tonic for a nervous heart
- Motherwort is a cardiac tonic
- Rosemary is good for palpitations
- Valerian is high in Magnesium which supports the nervous system

It is highly recommended that you consult a Naturopath or Herbalist if you choose to use herbs. Some herbs may be contraindicated with prescribed medicines. The safest way to use fresh herbs is as a brewed tea or in cooking.

Minerals

Leo people are determined, loyal, proud, bossy, dramatic, fun-loving, affectionate, generous, and egocentric. Leo usually have a strong body constitution but need to include exercise that supports their spine and back. Having a creative outlet soothes the spirit and gives their life meaning. Leo is prone to heart ailments, blocked arteries, ribs, eye disorders and back trouble.

Essential minerals - iodine, magnesium, potassium, sodium

Enriched food sources - seaweed, seafood, iodised salt, wholegrain cereals, wheat germ, pulses, nuts, sesame seeds, dried fruits, green vegetables, avocados, potatoes, anchovies and yeast extract.

Nutrition

Leo rules strength, vitality, the heart, the vertebrae, aorta, vena cava, coronaries, nerves and marrow of the spinal column, and thorax.

Common ailments include heart related ailments, palpitations, aneurysms from stress, sunstroke, muscular rheumatism, angina, fainting, high blood pressure, atherosclerosis, and thoracic back pain.

Beneficial foods include: Kelp, bran, carob, buckwheat, molasses, seafood, sunflower seeds, green veggies, chlorophyll, nuts, a little red meat, plums, beetroot, carrot, oranges, oats, asparagus, spinach, eggs, mangoes, and apples. Avoid stimulants, refined, processed and overheating foods.

Tissue Salt

Magnesium Phosphate is also known as Mag Phos.

When lacking magnesium phosphate Leos will exhibit an overactive mind, irritability, depression, stress, sharp headaches, angina, palpitations, cramps, menstrual pain, high cholesterol, tinnitus, shaking, spasm, and neuralgia.

Foods containing magnesium phosphate include almonds, apples, figs, wheat bread, barley, eggs, asparagus, cabbage, cucumber, walnuts, coconut, onions, and blueberries.

Vitamins

Foods containing essential vitamins suitable for Leo:

<u>A:</u>   Liver, carrots, parsley, sweet potato, spinach, mangoes, chives, tomatoes, and broccoli.

<u>C:</u>   Citrus fruits, red chilli peppers, kale, parsley, cauliflower, broccoli, turnip greens, sprouts, spinach, cabbage, mangoes, oysters, lima beans, strawberries, and raspberries.

<u>D:</u>   Fish liver oils, dairy, tuna, salmon, and sardines.

<u>E:</u>   Vegetable oil, wheat germ, soybeans, whole grains, raw nuts, raw seeds, and eggs.

> **Recommended Daily Health Tip**
> Add saffron to your meals as this is a great herb for the heart health.

Best Day and Number

Leo is ruled by the Sun and is governed by Sunday and the number 1.

Mantra

I give from my heart, so I need to support my heart health.

Personal Notes:

Virgo

August 23rd to September 22nd

Sign Profile

Virgos can be very analytical, critical, fickle, organised, objective, discriminating, modest, grounded, practical, helpful, and service orientated by nature.

Virgos are very service orientated. They like to help and often end up in hospitality or caring careers like nursing or social work. Their keen eye for detail and analytical minds makes them good at research and accounting.

Virgos body constitution is usually good as they are attracted to fresh whole foods. As their ruling planet is Mercury their health can be changeable depending on their mental state as this affects their digestion directly.

Virgos worry. Their energy is often used up by worrying about things they cannot control or change. This can affect their digestion and sleep patterns. It is important to do meditation or some other relaxation therapy for the mind. I recommend getting out of their head, doing something with their hands e.g. cooking, gardening or craft.

Virgos have a sensitive digestive system and often suffer with digestive disorders. Symptoms may include body weakness, constipation, diarrhoea, indigestion, malabsorption, offensive flatus, bloating nervous stomach and parasites. I recommend starting with a parasite cleanse (repeat in 3 months to kill any eggs, then annually), remove all sugar and white processed foods from diet, take prebiotic and probiotics, eat organic or fresh whole foods, drink lemon and warm water first thing in the morning, drink lots of filtered water, no coffee and exercise regularly.

Case Study

Vanessa came to see me with complaints of not sleeping well. Her insomnia was starting to affect her lifestyle and her work. She felt tired when she woke in the morning despite going to bed by 9:30pm most nights. I noticed she was exhibiting signs of irritability and impatience, both signs of sleep deprivation.

Her chart indicated an overactive Mercury (which rules Virgo) which was being aggravated by a transit as the primary cause. I recommended the following;

- Relaxation meditation 20 minutes before bed
- Be exposed to sunlight every day
- Reduce worry and stress
- Avoid cigarettes, coffee and Coca-Cola
- Evening meal should be light and eaten by 7pm
- Go for a light walk after meals
- Stop eating at least two hours before retiring
- Warmed milk with cinnamon or nutmeg to taste
- Warm oil massage to head and feet after warm lavender bath
- Your bedroom needs to have soothing colours. NO RED PLEASE AS THIS DISTURBS SLEEP
- Your bedroom should be well ventilated
- Soft music and slight fragrance may be used
- Apply lavender to the soles of your feet and temples at night
- Avoid the use of television and computer devices in your bedroom
- Have dim lighting in the evenings
- Best time to retire is between 9-10pm
- Melatonin or 5HTP with magnesium can be taken 30 minutes before bed

After discussion with me Vanessa understood that she needed to retrain her brain to achieve restful sleep. With the above guidelines, she developed a routine which she followed every night. This took a few weeks to take effect. Vanessa now reports she feels refreshed on waking and has more energy through the day.

When you are too much in your head, get into your hands. When working with your hands your brain has a chance to rest from being over analytical and worrying too much.

Associated Body Organs

- Upper Digestion
- Mental Nervous System
- Body parts affected include small intestines, pancreas, solar plexus, salivary glands, liver and bowels

Other body systems that need support to promote vitality for Virgos are: The Immune, Lymphatic system, Autonomic Nervous system, Respiratory and the Central Nervous system.

Virgos know when they are unbalanced because:

Virgos, when unbalanced worry too much. They worry about what they cannot change, worry about 'what if', and everything associated with their life. This behaviour contributes to insomnia and an overactive nervous system which can cause anxiety. They have high expectations and are known to be picky and hypercritical. Although usually very social by nature, when they are in a negative mind-set, they become aloof and sceptical.

How best to overcome Stress

Activities to Minimise Stress

As your mind is constantly active you need to learn to relax and calm your mind daily. A great practice for you is meditation, 20 minutes minimum. This practice will keep you focused, grounded, and aligned with life. You love to exercise your brain, reading, crosswords and brain teasers suit you. Remember you are trying to rest your mind so limit these activities.

Virgo needs to have a regular schedule to keep in shape. Exercise like Pilates, Yoga, Tai chi, gardening, walking in nature, rock climbing, hiking, cricket, tennis, darts, snooker, ballet, aerobics, Zumba, and gymnastics are all beneficial. They respond well to regular cleansing or a detoxification diet and natural therapies.

Charity work soothes the soul promoting a better sense of wellbeing.

Recommended Therapies

Aromatherapy

Signature Oil – Lavender
Lavender is a popular oil, most used for its antibacterial, balancing, relaxing, stimulant, antipyretic, analgesic, antispasmodic and wound healing properties. Lavender can ease the tendency to worry, soothe achy muscles and promote restful sleep.

Ayurveda

Dosha Constitution - Vata the air element. Primarily rules the lower abdomen, appendix, small intestines, assimilation of nutrients, and the lower digestive system.

Bach Flowers

Virgo - Centaury
Virgos live in their head most of the time and would really benefit from working with their hands to get them out of their head. Find out what they like to do: cooking, pottery, gardening, art, dance, Tai Chi, Yoga, and swimming would be excellent choices for this person. They worry about stuff they cannot change and fear they are not perfect enough and that this will disappoint others. Centaury allows them to be of service and not be taken for granted. They will hold their own in a healthy manner.

Chakra

Spiritual Chakra - Vishuddha
Virgo rules the throat, the fifth chakra. Virgos love to research, analyse, and categorise information that they can then share and communicate with other people.

Signs of imbalance include speech impediments, sore throat, cough, neck problems, laryngitis, thyroid imbalance, respiratory and/or hearing problems and lies.

Colour

<u>GREEN -</u> the colour of healing and balance
Positive-harmonious, balanced, sharing, protective and secure
Negative-insincere, selfish, jealous, threatened, and insecure

Balance negative vibrations by using more brown, purple, and white.

Affirmation- 'I am balanced, centred and secure in my thoughts.'

Crystals

<u>Carnelian</u> - promotes stimulation and motivation, strengthens creativity and is grounding.

Physically helps support metabolism, enhance memory, fertility, blood disorders, arthritis, lower back, depression, and headaches. Supports the circulatory, urinary, nervous systems and accelerates wound healing.

Herbs

- Alfalfa to aid protein digestion
- Brahmi an Ayurvedic herb, boosts memory and reduces mental fatigue
- Dill helps cleanse the digestive track of ulcerations
- Fennel to help balance digestion
- Slippery elm and peppermint to soothe digestion
- Vervain for the central nervous system

It is highly recommended that you consult a Naturopath or Herbalist if you choose to use herbs. Some herbs may be contraindicated with prescribed medicines. The safest way to use fresh herbs is as a brewed tea or in cooking.

Minerals

Virgos are adaptable, intelligent, critical, diligent, capable, worrisome, restless and analytical. They have a need to serve others; if this is at their expense, this will lead to disease. They must learn to serve themselves first in order to be healthy so then they can be of service to others. Prone to indigestion, mal-absorption, appendix, irritable bowel, colitis, allergy, weak nerves, spleen, and sluggish liver.

Essential minerals - magnesium, calcium, chloride, phosphorus, potassium, sodium

Enriched food sources - wholegrain cereals, wheat germ, pulses, nuts, sesame seeds, dried fruits, green vegetables, dairy, sardines, salt, avocados, potatoes, anchovies and yeast extract, green leafy vegetables, lean meat, poultry, fish and seafood.

Nutrition

Virgo rules pancreatic function, small intestine, nutrient absorption and assimilation, the spleen, enzyme production in the liver, mental health, intestinal and hepatic veins, and gastric arteries. Common ailments include: diabetes, hypoglycaemia, colitis, irritable bowel syndrome, poor nutrient assimilation, worry, nervous tension, pancreatitis, gastroenteritis, fatty liver, and weak intestinal peristalsis.

Beneficial foods include papaya, bitter greens, fennel, alfalfa, chicory, slippery elm powder, peppermint, endive, olives, oats, rye, rice bran, psyllium husks, apples, sprouts, figs, whole wheat, nuts and seeds. Avoid eating when nervous or stressed: meat, sweets, cakes and pastries, over processed foods.

Tissue Salt

Potassium Sulphate is also known as Kali Sulph.

When lacking in potassium sulphate Virgos will exhibit sinus, psoriasis, wet eczema, chronic tinea, itchy dry flaky skin, skin eruptions, yellow tinge on tongue, fuzzy head and will anger easily.

Foods containing potassium sulphate include carrot, oats, whole wheat, salad vegetables, rye, and chicory.

Vitamins

Foods containing essential vitamins suitable for Virgo:

B1: Pork, liver, heart, kidneys, fish, potatoes, nuts, pulses, rice bran, soy milk, rolled oats, lima beans, peas, lentils, and mung beans.

B complex: Leafy green vegetables and green fruits.

> **Recommended Daily Health Tip**
> Practice meditation as this help calm the mind and soothe the digestion.

Best Day and Number

Virgo is ruled by Mercury and is governed by Wednesday and the number 5.

Mantra

When I am too much in my head I need to get into my hands and be creative.

Personal Notes:

Libra

September 23rd to October 22nd

Sign Profile

Librans by nature are romantic, peace-making, charming, harmonious, over-pleasing, indecisive, lazy, idealistic, fair-minded, and tactful by nature.

Libras constitution is usually good but not robust. Having planet Venus as their ruler, they are attracted to all things sweet and indulgent. This increases heat in the body which is a catalyst for many health problems.

Many believe that the sign Libra is well balanced. This is a myth. Libra craves harmony, peace, and beauty. After all Libra rules all things romantic and beautiful. Librans will go out of their way to please others to maintain harmony. Unfortunately, this comes at a cost. By over pleasing in a need to be loved or accepted, they extend themselves to the point of resentment. This resentment brings ill health. Libra seeks love at any cost. They need to learn to accept and love themselves, so they attract healthy instead of dysfunctional relationships. When all aspects of their life are in harmony, only then is Libra in balance.

As mentioned, Libra has a lot to do with balance. Conditions affecting the inner ear cause unstable gait. Tinnitus is a condition which exhibits as vertigo, partial deafness, and ringing in ears. Home remedy herbal tea: equal amounts of comfrey, cinnamon, and chamomile. Steep up to 1 tsp of this mixture and drink 2-3 times a day. Gently rub warm sesame oil behind your ears twice daily. Limit environmental noise, reduce salt, caffeine, chocolate, and tea. Increase vitamin B, zinc, magnesium, and ginkgo to help reduce the noise and practice visualization with deep breathing for at least 10 mins daily.

Consult an acupuncturist, osteopath, or chiropractic as they can help with the alignment issues.

Case Study

Lucas, a young man in his thirties came to see me with lower back pain, low grade fever, pain when passing urine, low grade fever, fatigue, and mild nausea. He shared with me that he had gone to his doctor and was given antibiotics which did give some relief. As to the nature of the symptoms I asked about his sexual activity. He confirmed he was not sexually active and that this had been covered in his doctor's examination. I then asked if his urine was offensive in smell and he said it was. His astrological chart confirmed the problem was with his kidneys and his doctor was treating him for urinary tract infection. In combination with his medical treatment I recommended the following;

- Drink copious amounts of unsweetened cranberry, blueberry juice and water. This dilutes the urine and changes the PH of the urine, so bacteria are less likely to grow
- Magnesium Citrate 300-400mg daily helps keep urine alkaline that prohibits bacterial growth
- High dose Vitamin C with bioflavonoids and Vitamin A help strengthen the bladder wall making it harder for bacteria to stick to it
- Herb Uva-ursi kills bacteria in the urine
- If on antibiotics, you MUST TAKE probiotics
- An alkaline diet
- Avoid alcohol, coffee, spices, and heating foods
- Boiled ginger root for nausea
- Empty your bladder as soon as you feel the urge to urinate.

Urinary tract infections have a habit of returning even if you are on antibiotics. When your body is too acid it is easier for bacteria to return and grow. On my follow up with Lucas, he had remained on the fluid challenge, added probiotics, reported his urine was not offensive any longer and that the nausea and pain had subsided.

Associated Body Organs

- Endocrine System balances hormones
- Body parts affected include adrenal glands, kidneys, urethras, inner ear, bladder, lower lumbar region and thyroid.

Other body systems that need support to promote vitality for Libra sign are, the Muscular, Skeletal and the Lower Digestive system.

Librans know when they are unbalanced because:

Libra is all about the balance. Every aspect of their life needs stability in order to achieve harmony and inner balance. In a negative state Libra will exhibit being indecisive (more than usual), gullible, insincere, and lazy. Libra may become more dependent on others and indulge in an excess of shopping so they can feel good about themselves. Libra will continue having their hair and nails done as this reflects how good they look on the outside. On the inside they may hide feelings of low self-esteem and lack of self-love.

How best to overcome Stress

Minimising Stress

Libra is happy when all areas in life are in harmony with each other. This is a tall order and needs constant care to maintain this balance. Being aesthetic, you have a strong connection to music, fashion, and the visual arts, as they soothe the soul. Colour can be used effectively to soften and balance your living environment. Libra people are not hugely into exercise. If their motive is to improve their appearance in some way, then they will commit to an exercise routine. Otherwise they are better off with a person who will exercise with them. As they do not like to upset others, chances are they will commit to exercise if another person is involved.

Fresh air, meditation, Yoga, Tai Chi, being in relaxing environments and having stimulating interactions with others all serve you well. Exercises that benefit you include ice skating, long distance walking, badminton, cricket, ballroom dancing, gymnastics, and swimming.

It is important that you hold your own power and do not devalue yourself for the sake of peace. As important as peace is to you, over compromising yourself will only lead to resentment and eventually illness. Pamper yourself with massage and beauty treatments. Lymphatic drainage works well for you and be well hydrated drinking plenty of non-stimulating fluids, water, soups, juice, and herbal teas.

Recommended Therapies

Aromatherapy

Signature Oil - Geranium
Geranium's primary function is to balance, a key word for Librans. It acts as an antidepressant, aphrodisiac, hormone balancer, anti-inflammatory and insect repellent. Helps maintain calmness and equilibrium, with great benefits for beauty and female reproductive disorders.

Ayurveda

Dosha Constitution-Vata/Kapha, a combination of air and water element. Primarily rules the small and back of kidneys, lumbar area, bladder, ureters, ovaries, and endocrine system.

Bach Flowers

Libra - Scleranthus
Associated with seeing both sides of any situation and wanting to be fair and still remain popular causing confusion. This will help find balance and clear confusion in their life making good decisions. Will help soothe the nerves which will calm the mind and they will start to see beauty in their environment and themselves over time.

Chakra

<u>Spiritual Chakra - Anahata</u>
Ruled by the heart, the fourth chakra and you are more concerned with co-operation, balance, and mediation within relationships. By achieving this, love flows freely without always compromising yourself.

Signs of imbalance: all heart related diseases, high blood pressure, mistrust, holding onto past hurts, grief, co-dependency and unable to give and receive freely.

Colour

<u>PINK</u> - the colour of love and affection

Positive - calming, soothing, increases confidence, affectionate, harmonious, and loving.
Negative - smothering, sickly, overwhelmed, and stagnant.

Balance negative vibrations by using more orange, yellows, reds and burgundy.

Affirmation - 'I am full of confidence with an abundant of love for myself and others'

Crystals

<u>Pink Tourmaline</u> - sharpens insight, perception, strengthens creativity, gives relaxation and compassion. Inspires trust and safety in love.

Physically supports the endocrine, skin, heart and lung. It balances hormones, helps in dyslexia, diabetes, removal of blockages and aids in detoxification.

Herbs

- Alfalfa is high in vitamin B and celery supports acid balance
- Burdock for kidney weakness
- Cranberry reduces burning on urination and urinary tract infections
- Feverfew aids in strengthening and cleansing the kidneys
- Sarsaparilla and Kelp for hormonal balance
- Vitex Agnus Castus balances female hormones

It is highly recommended that you consult a Naturopath or Herbalist if you choose to use herbs. Some herbs may be contraindicated with prescribed medicines. The safest way to use fresh herbs is as a brewed tea or in cooking.

Minerals

Librans are charming, indecisive, refined, and social, intellectual, artistic, polite, co-operative, and friendly. Unless everything in their life is in balance, they can become off-centre with themselves, thus contributing to disease. To be in happy relationships they need to have an integrated relationship with themselves first. Prone to glandular disorders, lower back, electrolyte imbalance, hormone, kidney, bladder, and liver problems.

Essential minerals - iodine, chromium, copper, chloride, sodium, potassium.

Enriched food sources - seaweed, seafood, iodised salt, lean meat, liver, egg yolk, wholegrain cereals, cheese, nuts, seeds, cocoa, mushroom, avocados, potatoes, fresh and dried fruit.

Nutrition

Libra rules homeostasis, the kidneys, ureters, bladder, acid-alkaline metabolism, the endocrine glands, medulla oblongata and adrenal glands Common ailments include: nephritis, urinary infections, kidney tubule obstructions, uraemia, sugar related problems, toxaemia and acid-alkaline imbalance.

Beneficial foods include celery, apples, strawberries, lettuce, cucumber, melon, capsicum and lemons, kelp, walnuts, pecans, fish, nuts, seeds, whole grains, vegetable juices, berries, seaweed, brown rice and citrus: Avoid over indulgences in salt and rich foods so as not to throw out kidney balance and have adequate water during the day to keep kidneys flushed.

Tissue Salt

Sodium Phosphate is also known as Nat Phos.

When lacking sodium phosphate Librans will exhibit an acid tongue, heartburn, burping, digestive problems, gastric and urinary acidity, and stomach ulcers.

Foods containing sodium phosphate include carrot, celery, spinach, beets, corn, asparagus, apples, figs, strawberry, raisins, blueberry, oatmeal, almonds, wheat, fresh coconut, and unpolished rice.

Vitamins

Foods containing essential vitamins suitable for Libra:

<u>A:</u>   Liver, carrots, parsley, sweet potato, spinach, mangoes, chives, tomatoes, and broccoli

<u>B:</u>   Pork, liver, heart, kidneys, fish, potatoes, nuts, pulses, rice bran, soymilk, rolled oats, lima beans, peas, lentils, and mung beans

<u>B3:</u>   Milk, yoghurt, eggs, meat, poultry, and fish

<u>E:</u>   Vegetable oil, wheat germ, soybeans, whole grains, raw nuts, raw seeds, and eggs

<u>B complex:</u>   Leafy green vegetables and green fruits

<u>C:</u>   Citrus fruits, red chilli peppers, kale, parsley, cauliflower, broccoli, turnip greens, sprouts, spinach, cabbage, mangoes, oysters, lima beans, strawberries, and raspberries.

> **Recommended Daily Health Tip**
> Eat an alkaline diet. This will maintain the ph of the body and will maintain homeostasis.

Best Day and Number

Libra is ruled by Venus and is governed by Friday and the number 6.

Mantra

Positive, clear decisions promote good health.

Personal Notes:

Scorpio

October 23rd to November 21st

Sign Profile

Scorpio people are known as mysterious, magnetic, intense, sexual, powerful, psychic, emotional, secretive, passionate, introspective, stubborn, jealous, transformative, and controlling by nature.

Scorpios usually have strong constitutions. Holding onto past hurts will only deepen any illness. They need to move through their process by feeling the pain, understanding the lesson then letting it go. When unwell, Scorpios respond well to intensive treatments.

Planets Pluto and Mars have dual rulership over this sign. They both have domain over the reproductive system. It is not uncommon for Scorpio to suffer with health issues in that area sometime in their life. For women, take vitamins A, B and E, foods rich in calcium, magnesium, Rutin and herbs Dong Quai, pennyroyal, raspberry leaf to support the reproductive system. Caution should be taken with pennyroyal as too much can induce miscarriage. For men, a healthy diet and herbs Nettle root and Saw Palmetto that support the prostate.

It is highly recommended that you consult a Naturopath or Herbalist if you choose to use herbs. Some herbs may be contraindicated with prescribed medicines. The safest way to use fresh herbs is as a brewed tea or in cooking.

Case Study

Selena came to me with complaints of constipation and rectal bleeding. During our discussion she also revealed she suffered with headaches, bad breath, muscle cramps and offensive urine. I noticed she had dry lips and her tongue was dry. Rectal bleeding is a serious symptom. Selena confirmed she went to the doctors and the doctor felt the bleeding was due to straining when opening her bowels. Her chart indicated 3 planets in the sign of Scorpio as part of a fixed cross.

Selena also mentioned she only drank about 4 cups of water daily.

I recommended the following;

- A diet high in bran, fruit, and vegetables
- Adding fibre to a smoothie in the morning is good
- Have Aloe Vera, 20mls twice a day
- Psyllium husks, prune juice and magnesium are also useful
- Maintain regular exercise 4-5 times a week
- Have your main meal at lunch, eat light meals in the evening and add soups to your diet
- Kiwifruit, prunes, and fruits with the skin
- Avoid ice, coffee, smoking, alcohol, hot spicy foods, and breads as they slow down digestion.
- Increase your warm water intake
- Have warm water with lemon juice in the morning
- Soak your buttocks with Epsom salts in a bath, this will promote healing
- Increase water, herbal teas, soups, juice to 2.5 Litres daily
- Apply witch hazel externally for soothing
- Add Vitamin C, E, and zinc to diet to aid healing

On follow-up with Selena several weeks later, she confirmed everything was going well. She was having smooth evacuations, so I advised her to reduce her Aloe Vera to once daily in the morning. She was exercising 3 times a week and carried a 1 litre bottle of lemon water with her to work. She refilled the bottle at least once daily. Her bleeding had stopped.

Associated Body Organs

- Reproductive System
- Elimination System
- Body parts affected - pituitary gland, bones of the pelvis, large intestine, rectum, bladder, kidney, groin, prostate gland, sweat glands, genitalia and the nose and ears.

Other body systems that need support to promote vitality for Scorpio sign are, the Circulatory, Metabolic and the Cardiac system.

Scorpios know when they are unbalanced because:

Scorpio in a negative space is all about control, possessiveness, and intensity. They can hold a grudge till hell freezes over which is not ideal for good health. They will exhibit signs of being secretive, hold onto resentment, can be stubborn, suspicious, manipulative, and jealous. Scorpio has a good imagination and can often create the worst possible scenario and act on that scenario even if it isn't real.

How best to overcome Stress

<u>Minimising Stress</u>
As a Scorpio you approach life's challenges with natural intensity and an investigative mind. Scorpio can be very focused and driven in their endeavours. They need to get to the bottom of things, and once achieved, this gives them a sense of peace. Scorpio people enjoy this process although it appears to be stressful to others looking on.

Scorpio are competitive with others and with themselves; the following sports and exercises serve you best: Yoga, shooting, fencing, swimming, scuba diving, fishing, running, canoeing, weightlifting, kickboxing, and boxing. Sex is also a great outlet, and if you are not having sex then sports needs to be a primary focus in your life so you have a channel for your high energy levels. Remember, sex is not competitive.

Music and the arts are nurturing for the Scorpio soul allowing emotions to form a synergy inducing calmness and relaxation. Having an investigative tendency, they are often drawn to metaphysics, the occult, and the study of the mind.

Living close to or being exposed to the ocean soothes their soul. Learn to laugh more as this promotes immunity. Colonic therapies on a regular basis suit your constitution well. (Seek Medical advice before commencement).

Recommended Therapies

Aromatherapy

Signature Oil - Patchouli
Patchouli is primarily an aphrodisiac, decongestant, antidepressant, regenerative and antiseptic. Powerfully potent, in South East Asia, this oil used to treat snake bites and poisonous insects, hence the healing effect of this oil.

Ayurveda

Dosha Constitution
- Kapha/Pitta, the water and fire element. Primarily rules the colon, bowel, sacrum, anus, prostrate, bladder, urethra, external sex organs, sexual vitality, and the reproductive elimination systems.

Bach Flowers

Scorpio-Chicory
Associated with being self-indulgent, always being right, seeking attention, jealousy, and possessiveness if they do not feel secure. This will help not be so self-critical and will help reduce thoughts associated with fear and panic. Promotes generosity while allowing for individual freedom.

Chakra

Spiritual Chakra - Manipura
Scorpios are also linked to the third chakra, situated in the solar plexus, but unlike Aries, Scorpios tend to have issues with power struggles and understanding power; usually through sexual, physical, emotional, or mental abuse. Their role is to transcend the lesson and transmute the power to empower the self. Once they have done this for themselves Scorpio can then become a facilitator for other people's healing.

Colour

MAROON - the colour of passion and strength

Positive - compassionate, loving, genuine, mature, supportive
Negative - unkind, selfish, artificial, stubborn, unhelpful

Balance negative vibrations by using more greens, pinks, blue and purple.

Affirmation - 'I am centred in my own personal power and respect the personal power of others.'

Crystals

Malachite — relieves stress, aids expression, extends patience, restores emotional balance and helps maintain discipline.

Physically detoxifies liver and gallbladder, helps with insomnia, allergies, eyes, cramps, menstrual problems, blood pressure, arthritis, joints, epilepsy, vertigo, high acid. Also supports the immune and circulatory systems.

Herbs

- Aloe Vera and Senna as laxatives for constipation
- Dong Quai, pennyroyal, raspberry leaf to support the reproductive system
- Nettle root and Saw Palmetto supports the prostate
- Valerian is calming and supports the nerves and bowel
- Wormwood clears parasites from the bowel, should be done annually
- Yellow dock and calendula for lymphatics and detoxification

It is highly recommended that you consult a Naturopath or Herbalist if you choose to use herbs. Some herbs may be contraindicated with prescribed medicines. The safest way to use fresh herbs is as a brewed tea or in cooking.

Minerals

Scorpio people are intense, magnetic, sexy, determined, intuitive, powerful, controlling, loyal, possessive, and emotional. Being unable to let go of past hurts and betrayal can often contribute to disease. Scorpio need to understand their personal power and learn how to use it constructively with themselves and others. Prone to prostate gland trouble, sexually transmitted disease, haemorrhoids, colitis, bladder, cystitis, constipation, inguinal hernia, and menstrual issues.

Essential minerals - selenium, iron, copper, zinc
Enriched food sources - lean meat, fish, dairy, brazil nuts, avocado, lentils, sardines, dark green leafy vegetables, shellfish, nuts seeds, mushroom, cocoa, wholegrain cereals, oysters, peanuts, and sunflower seeds.

Nutrition

Scorpio mainly rules reproduction and the elimination process, the bowel, sweat glands, nose with regard to release of toxins, sphincter of the bladder, rectum and external genitalia. Common ailments include: constipation, haemorrhoids, diseases of the reproductive system, prostate gland, womb disorders, menstrual irregularities, seminal complaints, spasms in the colon connected to emotional distress, growths in the colon and sluggish peristalsis.

Beneficial foods include fresh fruit and veggies, lemon, apple cider vinegar, kelp, garlic, prunes, onions, molasses, grapefruit, whole grains, nuts, wheat germ, oats, brown rice, figs, apples, and water. Avoid fermented and mucus forming foods, heating, and stimulating foods, meat and salty foods.

Tissue Salt

Calcium Sulphate is also known as Calc Sulph.

When lacking calcium sulphate Scorpios will exhibit irritability, moodiness, pimples, boils, abscesses, ulcers, purulent discharge, wax build up, burning and itchy soles of feet.

Foods containing calcium sulphate include: asparagus, garlic, mustard, cress, turnips, cauliflower, radishes, leeks, onion, figs, prunes, black cherries, blueberries, coconut and gooseberries.

NEVER USE CALCIUM SULPHATE WITH SILICA.

Vitamins

Foods containing essential vitamins suitable for Scorpio:

<u>Complex B</u>: Leafy green vegetables and green fruits.

<u>C</u>: Citrus fruits, red chilli peppers, kale, parsley, cauliflower, broccoli, turnip greens, sprouts, spinach, cabbage, mangos, oysters, lima beans, strawberries, and raspberries.

<u>E</u>: Vegetable oil, wheat germ, soybeans, whole grains, raw nuts, raw seeds, and eggs.

<u>Folic acid</u>: Chicken beef livers, asparagus, lettuce, broccoli, fresh orange juice, legumes, and dark leafy green vegetables.

> ### <u>Recommended Daily Health Tip</u>
> Take Aloe Vera juice in the morning. This is a mild laxative and will help prevent constipation.

Best Day and Number
Scorpio is ruled by Mars and Pluto is governed by Tuesday and the number 9.

Mantra
The quicker I process, the more I understand the truth.

Personal Notes:

Sagittarius

November 22nd to December 21st

Sign Profile

Sagittarius are optimistic, enthusiastic, inspirational, fun loving, seek justice, expansive, easy going, generous, irresponsible, extremist, wasteful, conceited, and freedom loving by nature.

The health of a Sagittarian is usually robust. They are very active and are usually sporty, adventurous and love to travel. Their Achilles heel is they believe they are invincible and their ruling planet Jupiter, gives the energy of 'living life to the max'. Due to this belief system, they are not good at looking after their own health and tend to overindulge in life and food which can often lead to disease.

Sciatica is a common complaint. The sciatic nerve runs from the spine down the back of each leg. When surrounding tissues are inflamed there is intense spasm type pain and mobility is reduced. Keeping warm, bedrest, having warm baths with Epsom salts, warm oil massage, magnesium, alkaline diet, acupressure, and acupuncture are beneficial. Avoid meat, coffee, cheese, sugar, fish, cakes, puddings, and bread during the acute phase. You may benefit from Boswellia and Turmeric as they both anti-inflammatory in nature.

Case Study

Sam came to see me after he had consulted with his doctor about his liver. His blood results had come back with elevated liver markers and he wanted to treat his liver holistically. We discussed his diet and alcohol intake and he confessed he tended to overindulge. Sam mentioned he did not deal with his anger well. He tended to have outbursts which he regretted later. After further discussion around the importance of digestion and its effect on the liver, I recommended the following;

- Lemon juice in warm water first thing in morning. Good for liver and digestion
- Have your main meal at noon
- Drinks fluids 20 minutes either side of meals
- Have apple cider vinegar or lemon juice and warm water 5-10 minutes before meals.
- Drink decaffeinated coffee and teas
- Cook with coconut oil and drink coconut water
- Have an alkaline based diet
- Eat antioxidant foods e.g. berries, spinach, eggs, carrots, beets, broccoli, bright coloured vegetables and fruits
- Omega 3 oils decrease inflammation e.g. chia seeds, fish, some grains
- NOTE OMEGA 6 OILS increase inflammation in the body so limit vegetable oil, cakes and biscuits
- Avoid alcohol, spicy foods, sugar, butter, hard cheeses, white bread and meats high in fats
- Learn how to manage your anger in a productive manner
- Develop a philosophy of healthy living

Suggestions for liver detox
- Have 1 day where you just have fluids. NO coffee, tea (herbal teas ok), alcohol, fizzy drinks, or processed juice
- Herbal teas, infused water with mint, lemon and cucumber is good, broths, light soups, filtered water with lemon, coconut water and vegetable juice.
- Celery and beetroot juices
- If you get hungry during this time, having some grilled or steamed fish with lemon is ok
- Liver support should ideally be done in Spring and Autumn
- Dandelion tea or coffee is good to drink daily as a liver support
- Herbs you can take to support the liver include: milk thistle, turmeric, chicory, globe artichoke, peppermint and yellow dock root.

Sam reported back to me after his next doctor's appointment. He was happy as his liver function tests results were within normal limits. He also noticed he was digesting his food much better and he had more energy.

Associated Body Organs

- Motor Nervous System.
- Autonomic Nervous System.
- Body parts affected include liver, pancreas, spleen, hips, thighs, legs, buttocks, pelvis, pelvic muscles, sacrum, sacral spine, and sciatic nerve.

Other body systems that need support to promote vitality for Sagittarius sign are, the Immune, Lymphatic, Upper Digestion, Respiratory and the Central Nervous system.

Sagittarians know when they are unbalanced because:

Sagittarius is known for being 'happy go lucky' but when unbalanced will exhibit signs of irresponsibility, being tactless, dictatorial, and conceited. Sagittarius is famous for seeing the 'big picture' but they can go 'over the top'. In this state they can be wasteful due to over expanding their vision to the extreme. They will truly believe that it 'will work' as their belief in themselves or their project will have no boundaries. It will be difficult to stick to the agreed plan as Sagittarius will forge ahead oblivious to reality.

How best to overcome Stress

Minimising Stress
Sagittarians are freedom seekers and love being outdoors. As a fire sign they are very active and restless. For them, activity is a means of reducing stress. Suitable sports to channel their energy include horse riding, polo, skiing, archery, karate, bike riding, shooting, hockey, football, basketball and running.

As a Sagittarian, their mind can be as active as their body. They enjoy exploring the deeper meaning to life through philosophy, reading and higher learning. Meditation and deep breathing exercises like Tai Chi and Yoga benefit your sign.

Sagittarius has a tendency to live life in extremes. Having regular gallbladder and liver detoxification helps to rejuvenate your body. (Seek medical advice before commencement).

Recommended Therapies

Aromatherapy

Signature Oil - Black Pepper
Black Pepper is fiery oil, it stimulates, tones muscles, and is carminative. This oil gets straight to the root and will relieve a tired mind or painful stiff muscles.

Ayurveda

Dosha Constitution - Pitta/Kapha, the fire and water elements. Primarily rules the arteries, liver, pancreas, hips, thighs, sciatica, and the autonomic nervous system.

Bach Flowers

Sagittarius – Agrimony
Associated with mental worry but puts on a jovial mask to the world. Distressed by argument they hide their pain behind humour. Feeling nervous about the future they often escape into recreational drugs. They need lots of space to process. Agrimony will help them deal with reality and not escape it. Will aid in bringing a positive attitude and renewed faith. Also helps to bring inner and outer peace and harmony.

Chakra

<u>Spiritual Chakra - Svadhisthana</u>
Linked to the second chakra in the sacral area, this is primarily concerned with expansion, creative expression and pleasure, emotional and sexual balance within relationships.

Signs of imbalance lower back pain, reproductive complaints, bladder, kidney troubles, imbalanced sex drive, guilt, feelings of isolation and emotional instability.

Colour

<u>ROYAL BLUE</u> - the colour of royalty and authority

Positive-calm, tranquil, honest, accepting, reassuring, peaceful
Negative-depressed, withdrawn, distrusting, inflexible, isolated

Balance negative vibrations by using more orange, greens, royal blue and purple.

Affirmation- 'I am attaining more peace and tranquillity in my life.'

Crystals

<u>Turquoise</u> - brings communication to emotional issues, very grounding, induces wisdom, understanding and brings friendship and self-realization.

Physically supports tissue regeneration, neutralises acid, immune system, works well with mood swings, depression, panic attacks and is anti-inflammatory.

Herbs

- Agrimony tones the liver
- Burdock - which is cooling and is a blood cleanser
- Celery for arthritis especially in the hips
- Dandelion and Chicory cleanses an overheated blood system which cools the liver
- Milk thistle protects and repairs liver cells
- Turmeric is excellent as an antioxidant and anti-inflammatory for the liver

It is highly recommended that you consult a Naturopath or Herbalist if you choose to use herbs. Some herbs may be contraindicated with prescribed medicines. The safest way to use fresh herbs is as a brewed tea or in cooking.

Minerals

Sagittarius are optimistic, outspoken, freedom loving, truth seeking, affectionate, adventurous, quick tempered, lively, humorous, sporty, and inconsistent. They are prone to overindulgence of food, drink, sex, exercise, and gambling. This can cause health problems from their forties onwards if not well controlled. They are truth seekers; they seek wisdom from life.

Prone to sciatica, fever, gout, liver disorders, diabetes, arthritis, hip and thigh disorders.
Essential minerals-chromium, zinc, manganese
Enriched food sources- oysters, peanuts, sunflower seeds, red meat, liver, egg yolk, seafood, cheese, nuts, brown rice, whole grain breads and cereals.

Nutrition

Sagittarius rules the hips, thighs, sciatic nerve, muscle coordination, the liver, buttocks, pelvis and lumbar region. Common ailments include sciatica, injury to coccyx, gout, hip and thigh disorders, sclerosis, hepatitis, liver congestion, hip and pelvic ailments, nervous system disorders and diabetes.

Beneficial foods include mushrooms, whole grains, brewer's yeast, whole eggs, wheat germ and shellfish; apples including skin, alfalfa, kelp, rye, figs, rice, cucumber, berries, prunes and cherries; Lettuce, corn, endive, chicory, onions, asparagus and horseradish. Avoid overindulging, acid forming foods, and over exertion physically and mentally.

Tissue Salt

Silica is also known as Silicea.

When lacking silica Sagittarians will exhibit anxiety, blind acne, sties, sweaty smelly feet, abnormal calcification of bone, tendons, ligaments and cartilage, fungal growth, sleepwalking and white spots on nails.

Foods containing silica include edible skins on all fruit and vegetables, prunes, figs, and strawberries.

NEVER USE SILICA IF YOU HAVE METAL PINS AND PLATES IN YOUR BODY.

Vitamins

Foods containing essential vitamins suitable for Sagittarius:

<u>B6:</u> Lean meat, poultry, fish, eggs, whole wheat breads and cereals, nuts, bananas, soybeans, brown rice, lentils, lima beans, avocados, spinach, potatoes, cauliflower, popcorn, and leeks.

<u>C</u>: Citrus fruits, red chilli peppers, kale, parsley, cauliflower, broccoli, turnip greens, sprouts, spinach, cabbage, mangoes, oysters, lima beans, strawberries, and raspberries.

Recommended Daily Health Tip
For liver health take lemon juice with warm water every morning.

Best Day and Number

Sagittarius is ruled by Jupiter and is governed by Thursday and the number 3.

Mantra

For a long life, all things in moderation.

Personal Notes:

Capricorn

December 22nd to January 19th

Sign Profile

Capricorns are known as disciplined, ambitious, serious, committed, studious, responsible, strict, calculating, conservative, dutiful, practical, and hardworking by nature. The constitution of a Capricorn in childhood is usually weak. As they grow and mature their constitution becomes very strong.

Planet Saturn rules Capricorn which has domain over structures and boundaries. This is the reason: the skeletal system and skin are primarily affected.

Many people who have strong Capricorn placements in their astrology charts suffer with conditions of the bone. Bone support is crucial in maintaining wellbeing. Recommendations include; monitoring their Vitamin D and calcium levels; low impact exercise like walking on flat ground; alkaline, vegetarian and Mediterranean diets are helpful; ingest good oils, avocados and flaxseed oil, include Vitamins B, C, D, K2, calcium and magnesium. Sunshine 20 mins daily is beneficial.

Case Study

Caroline came to me with symptoms of foggy memory, irritability, feelings of sadness, low energy levels, and insomnia. After an assessment of astrology her chart, I noticed she was born with planet Saturn in aspect at the midpoint of her Sun and Moon. This can indicate depression. Caroline confirmed that she went through phases, sometimes feeling good, sometimes not so good. I asked her what her vitamin D level was, and she said she had never had the blood test done. I recommended the following:

- St. John's Wort (Hypericum) is uplifting, contraindicated in lactation. (May interact with some prescribed medications). **DO NOT TAKE ST JOHNS WORT IF ALREADY ON ANTIDEPRESSANTS.** If on oral contraceptives, St. John's wort may reduce the effectiveness of the pill.

- Valerian, chamomile, sleepy time tea, warm milk with nutmeg or cinnamon for sleep
- Increase raw fruits and vegetables, cereals, green leafy vegetables, and whole grains
- Decrease intake of dairy and fat
- Avoid coffee, coca cola and fizzy drinks
- Include mango, passionfruit, seafood, brazil nuts and spinach which are natural mood elevators
- Drink lemon balm daily for anxiety
- Increase Vitamin B especially B2, B6, iron, magnesium, zinc and vitamin C
- Increase your fish oils, omega 3 fatty acids
- Brazil nuts, grains, chicken, turkey, peas, soybeans, organic honey, and liquorice are natural antidepressants
- Acupuncture and deep breathing
- Avoid black, blue, browns or dark colours as they depress the immune system
- Wear light colours only, green, yellow, reds, orange, purples, pinks and white
- Walk barefoot on grass or beach for grounding
- Sunshine 20 minutes daily and exercise
- Essential oils orange, rose, geranium, lavender, or bergamot in a burner or apply externally
- Listen and sing to upbeat music
- Turn negative thoughts into positive action
- Use positive affirmations
- Share how you feel with someone you trust
- Cry when needed to release blocks
- Have a massage as often as you can
- Keep a diary; be creative: paint, dance, or sing
- Watch comedy and laugh often
- Stay away from people in crisis
- Learn to say NO and mean it when necessary
- Pamper yourself weekly
- MOST IMPORTANT have a Vitamin D blood test

Caroline followed up with me once she had been to her doctor. She reported that her vitamin D was very low, and her iron was below normal. This made sense as a low vitamin D is often linked to depression. Low iron levels mean she was not getting enough oxygen to her brain which explained her poor memory. Vitamin D and iron were corrected and was checked closely by her doctor. Caroline started to feel better and incorporated many of the recommendations we discussed as part of her daily routine.

Associated Body Organs

- Skeletal System
- Body parts affected: skin, bones, body joints, knees, hair, nails, teeth, gallbladder, and parathyroid gland.

Other body systems that need support to promote vitality for Capricorn sign are, the Muscular, Adrenal, Endocrine, Urinary and the Lower Digestive system.

Capricorns know when they are unbalanced because:

Capricorn is strong and reliable in a balanced state. When under stress they will exhibit intolerance, show signs of mistrust, may choose to separate themselves from others and can be introverted. Depression is often associated with Capricorn when they turn in on themselves over long periods of time. It takes time for this sign to come out of their misery and may remain despondent until they do.

How best to overcome Stress

Minimising Stress
Capricorns are very serious by nature and need to bring more laughter and fun into their life. Both these things improve their immunity. A dose of 20 minutes of sunshine daily improves their skin and sense of wellbeing.

Regular exercise like Yoga, Pilates, gardening, golf, cricket, skiing, running and snooker improves circulation. They are ambitious and do well in activities like Ironman and rock climbing. They need a goal; this will spur them on in life.

In order to be a success, sometimes Capricorns need to go with the flow more. Capricorn likes to be alone and can often sit and read as a form of relaxation. Listening to music or singing will also soothe you. If feeling dark and down, avoid black and dark colours as they sap your energy. Wear soothing greens and earth tones or motivating colours of oranges, and yellows. Psychotherapy, chiropractor, oil massage and osteopathy are beneficial therapies for you.

Recommended Therapies

Aromatherapy

Signature Oil - Vetivert
Vetivert known as the 'oil of tranquillity', aids the worrisome mind. It is grounding, antiseptic, relaxant, a woman's hormone balancer, aphrodisiac, and is regenerative. Works well on rheumatic and arthritic joint pain which Capricorns know about only too well.

Ayurveda

Dosha Constitution - Pitta/Vata, the fire and water elements. Primarily rules the skin, gallbladder, bones, knees, joints, teeth, ligaments, hair, nails and the skeletal system.

Bach Flowers

Capricorn - Mimulus
This will help face fear in daily life, fear of the unknown, feelings of insecurity and the pain associated with thoughts that accompany them. Everything in life is serious. They are ambitious and feel grief when they, in their view, fail other people. Mimulus gives Capricorn the faith that all will be well.

Chakra

Spiritual Chakra - Muladhara
Capricorns are ambitious and by nature work very hard so it's natural that they are linked to the first chakra found in the base of the spine. The lessons are around creating foundations for life, survival, security, providing for physical needs, grounding, health and standing up for what you believe in.

Signs of imbalance include constipation, obesity, leg and knee problems, osteoarthritis, incapable of being still and fear.

Colour

BLACK - the colour of grounding and protection

Positive - power, authority, respectable, sexy, strengthens.
Negative - depressed, death, rebellious, grief, withdrawn.

Balance negative vibrations by using more orange, yellows, greens and whites.

Affirmation- 'I am feeling stronger and more powerful daily.'

Crystals

Obsidian - induces creativity and provides insight. Gives strength with compassion and helps to understand things that are hard to accept.

Physically helps with removal of blocks, detoxification, arthritis, joint pain, cramp, bleeding, prostate and circulatory problems.

Herbs

- Comfrey is suitable for bone repair and assisting with skin complaints
- Glucosamine and Chondroitin nourish the joints, improving movement
- Heartsease soothes the skin that has eczema
- St John's Wort soothes the nervous system and helps with mild depression *(do NOT use if on antidepressants)*
- Willow bark, Boswellia, Devils claw, and turmeric are natural anti-inflammatory and pain relievers
- Wintergreen is a helpful treatment for rheumatism in the joints

It is highly recommended that you consult a Naturopath or Herbalist if you choose to use herbs. Some herbs may be contraindicated with prescribed medicines. The safest way to use fresh herbs is as a brewed tea or in cooking.

Minerals

Capricorns by nature are earthy, cold, and dry. They are dutiful, serious, practical, ambitious, hardworking, security conscious, wise, cautious, moralistic and sensual. All work and no play make for a dull unbalanced individual. They believe that they need to suffer to achieve goals in life. This is not healthy for the body. Try to be more spontaneous. Prone to skin disorders, fractures, dislocations, depression, melancholy, bad knees, dental and skeletal disorders.

Essential minerals - calcium, fluoride, magnesium, phosphorus, sulphur, manganese, molybdenum

Enriched food sources - dairy, sardines, green leafy vegetables, sesame seeds, tea, tap water (for fluoride), wholegrain cereals, wheat germ, pulses, nuts, lean meat, poultry, fish, brown rice, liver, yeast and wholegrain bread.

Nutrition

Capricorn rules the joints, knees, the skin, the skeletal system, tendons, cartilage and ligaments, the hair, nails, teeth, parathyroid gland, and gallbladder. Common ailments include skin disorders, rheumatism, arthritic complaints, problems with the synovial fluid of joints, gout, psoriasis, gallstones, bursitis, gallbladder, associated digestive disturbances, and irregular calcium metabolism.

Beneficial foods include: sardines, salmon, egg yolk, shellfish, nuts, sesame seeds, green leafy veggies, molasses, carob, legumes, essential fatty acids, nuts and seeds, oily fish and linseed (flaxseed) oil, kelp and dairy products. Heating, stimulating foods as well as foods that are well cooked are best absorbed. Avoid meat and acid forming foods.

Tissue Salt

Calcium Phosphate is also known as Calc Phos.

When lacking Calcium phosphate Capricorns will exhibit irritability, poor food absorption, poor appetite, cramps, slow development of muscles and bone, chilblains, cold feet, numbness in limbs and flatulence.

Foods containing Calcium phosphate include asparagus, spinach, cucumber, coconut, lettuce, lentils, beans, rye, barley, wheat, sea fish, cow's milk, figs, strawberries, plums, and blueberries.

Vitamins

Foods containing essential vitamins suitable for Capricorn:

A: Liver, carrots, parsley, sweet potato, spinach, mangos, chives, tomatoes, and broccoli.

C: Citrus fruits, red chilli peppers, kale, parsley, cauliflower, broccoli, turnip greens, sprouts, spinach, cabbage, mangoes, oysters, lima beans, strawberries, and raspberries.

D: Fish liver oils, tuna, salmon, sardines and dairy.

K: Broccoli, cabbage, and sprouts.

Bioflavonoid: Fresh vegetables, green peppers, grapes, apricots, strawberries, cherries, prunes, and blackcurrants

> **Recommended Daily Health Tip**
> Take Vitamin D daily as it is needed to absorb calcium into bones.

Best Day and Number

Capricorn is ruled by Saturn and is governed by Saturday and the number 4.

Mantra

I am always moving forward in a positive way.

Personal Notes:

Aquarius

January 20th to February 18th

Sign Profile

Aquarius are innovative, intellectual, impulsive, detached, independent, creative, futuristic, rebellious, unpredictable, unconventional, humanitarian and freedom loving by nature.

Aquarius ruled by planets Uranus and Saturn, are not great planners. This also applies to their diet and health routines. Due to their 'eat on the run' philosophy and their erratic nature, their constitution is often variable.

In order to maintain their health, Aquarians need to develop a practice that works for them. A couple of options are to take portable healthy foods so they can eat when they wish, eating bananas daily, which are high in potassium and magnesium, vital for nerve function. They also benefit from having healthy smoothies as they are full of nutrients.

If their circulatory system is depleted, this will directly affect the heart as the two systems are connected. Practising good heart health will contribute to keeping Aquarius happy and healthy.

Case Study

Adam came to see me complaining of cold hands and feet. He is an Aquarian, so I knew his circulatory system was the culprit. He was diagnosed with Raynaud's Syndrome and was seeking natural options to improve his condition. This disorder can indicate an underlying heart problem, so I asked about his heart health. He said he had stopped smoking 2 years ago and said his heart was fine, but he did have low blood pressure and experienced dizziness at times. After further discussing the connection with an adequate fluid intake and its effect on circulation, I recommended the following:

- Turmeric, fish oils and over-the-counter aspirin to thin the blood to aid circulation
- Vitamin B6 and B12, Vitamin C, Vitamin E, niacin, and magnesium
- Regular walking, swimming, or biking 20-30 mins a day in the sun
- Warming spices like cayenne, cinnamon, turmeric, ginger, cardamom, and curry to help stimulate heat in the body
- Herbs: Gingko, rosemary, Hawthorne (especially good for the heart)
- Foods including garlic, green tea, dark chocolate, coconut oil, nuts, tomato, onion
- A warm bath or foot spa will help with blood flow
- Wear red socks or long pants
- Low fat high fibre diet, no coffee, tea or alcohol and sugar products
- Keep cholesterol at normal levels
- Wear support stockings and comfortable shoes
- Increase fluid intake to 2.5 litres a day to maintain blood pressure

Adam added many of my recommendations to his daily routine with good results. He made sure his heart and blood pressure were checked every time he saw his doctor as there was a family history of heart disease, he discovered. By increasing his daily fluid intake, he noticed his dizziness had been reduced.

Associated Body Organs

- Circulatory System
- Body parts affected hypothalamus, parathyroid, eyes, ankles, legs, nervous system, the meridian system, the chakras and spinal cord.

Other body systems that need support to promote vitality for the Aquarius sign are the Reproductive, Elimination, Metabolic and the Cardiac system.

Aquarians know when they are unbalanced because:

Aquarius enjoys being the maverick of the Zodiac. When unsettled they can become erratic, rebellious, irritable, ungrounded, unpredictable, and eccentric. Aquarians are usually social but under stress they will be impersonal and seek refuge in separating out and being on their own. They love and need their own space in order to process problems and life in general. Usually friendly with others, when stressed they can be tactless and aloof.

How best to overcome Stress

Minimising Stress

Aquarius is very intellectual and they like spending time alone. They will often spend time reading or surfing the net to relax. Other people often see this as work and do not realise that this is how they unwind. Activities like chess, bridge, crosswords, and Sudoku that involve strategy of the mind often attract them. They enjoy affiliating with computer and technology groups. Having an inventive mind, you often like to dabble with electrical gadgets and technology. Space: the final frontier - this is another dimension you like to get absorbed and lost in. You do like music and dancing but usually it's to your own unique taste.

When you choose to get physical, sports that benefits are flying, parachuting, hang-gliding, badminton, skiing, ice skating, indoor climbing, and cycling. You are very much a team player, so most team sports do well for you. You love being free and nature gives you space and no limitations. Being in nature soothes your mind and keeps you grounded especially if you are working the land or are with animals. It is important to you that you live your unique lifestyle in order to be happy. Add a water feature to your home environment to soothe your nerves and help you connect to your emotions.

Beneficial therapies include meditation, acupuncture, homeopathy, and energy healing.

Recommended Therapies

Aromatherapy

<u>Signature Oil - Neroli</u>
Neroli oil is an aphrodisiac, antidepressant; is calmative, meditative, antispasmodic, and antiseptic. Works well on the mind giving confidence with strength and is great in the treatment of insomnia.

Ayurveda

<u>Dosha Constitution</u> - Vata/Pitta, the air and fire elements. Primarily rules the ankles, calves, veins, nerve impulses and the circulatory system.

Bach Flowers

<u>Aquarius - Water Violet</u>
Independent, intelligent, innovative and has a great desire to be alone. Being alone helps them to process life and their emotions. Clever and very talented once they recognise and channel their difference as a gift and do not try to "fit in". Water Violet is soothing and promotes inner peace.

Chakra

<u>Spiritual Chakra -Muladhara</u>
Linked to the first chakra, found in the base of the spine, the lessons are with creating foundations, survival, security, providing for physical needs, grounding, health and standing up for yourself. As Aquarians love their freedom, they frequently have a dilemma to be responsible in daily life and being free to be who they want to be. The secret is to have a life which can honour both happily.

Signs of imbalance include constipation, obesity, leg and knee problems, osteoarthritis, lower leg circulatory problems, incapable of being still and fear.

Colour

<u>PURPLE</u> - the colour of intuition and spirituality

Positive - intuitive, dignified, valuable, revealed, open-minded
Negative - hidden, humble, unworthy, alone, narrow-minded

Balance negative vibrations by using more orange, greens, browns and white.

Affirmation - 'I am naturally gifted and move forward with confidence.'

Crystals

<u>Fluorite</u> - conveys impartial, unbiased reasoning with detachment. Enables you to see the truth and reality behind illusion. Heightens mental abilities improving memory and concentration.

Physically supports coordination, joint ailments, dental work, neuralgia, digestion and assimilation of nutrients, disorders to bone, wound ulcers, and respiratory disease.

Herbs

- Brahmi improves memory and a nervous system tonic
- Garlic and Echinacea which increases immunity
- Ginkgo enhances blood circulation
- Silica to insulate the nerves (*do NOT use if you have metal implants inside your body*)
- St. John's Wort supports the nerves (*do NOT use with antidepressants or the contraceptive pill as it reduces its effect*)
- Rue and Mugwort for varicose veins

It is highly recommended that you consult a Naturopath or Herbalist if you choose to use herbs. Some herbs may be contraindicated with prescribed medicines. The safest way to use fresh herbs is as a brewed tea or in cooking.

Minerals

Aquarians are detached, humane, cool, original, intelligent, stubborn, gifted, eccentric and unemotional. Too much mental activity can cause damage to their central nervous system causing diseases in those areas. They need to cultivate their emotions through creative expression to give balance to their lives. Prone to ankle injuries, varicose veins, cramps, nervous disorders, blood and circulatory disorders of the legs and ankles.

Essential minerals - magnesium, potassium, sodium

Enriched food sources - whole grain cereals, wheat germ, pulses, nuts, green vegetables, salt, avocados, potatoes, fresh and dried vegetables.

Nutrition

Aquarius rules the calves, circulation, ankles, veins, nerve impulses, energy flow in the body, the eyes, spinal cord, the nadi energy system, and the oxygenation process. Common ailments include poor circulation, blood disorders, lower leg cramping, varicose veins, cataracts, glaucoma, multiple sclerosis, myelitis, nerve related muscular dystrophy, oedema, sprained ankles, spinal curvature, nerve degeneration, weak eyesight, anaemia and heart weakness.

Beneficial foods: ginger, onion, garlic, spices, and warming foods. Nerve relaxants such as essential fatty acids, nuts, seeds, fish, brewer's yeast, wheat germ, spinach, celery, root veggies, cheese, broccoli, apricots, peaches, eggs, lecithin, berries, and leafy green veggies. Avoid large amounts of salt.

Tissue Salt

Sodium Chloride is also known as Nat Mur.

When lacking sodium chloride Aquarians will exhibit hay fever, cold extremities, clear and runny mucus, sunstroke; they are pessimistic, sad, have pain in the eyes, tingling sensations, palms hot and perspiring.

Foods containing sodium chloride include carrots, cucumber, spinach, lettuce, coconut, lentils, chestnuts, asparagus radish, apples, figs, and strawberries.

Vitamins

Foods containing essential vitamins suitable for Aquarius:

<u>A</u>: Liver, carrots, parsley, sweet potato, spinach, mangoes, chives, tomatoes, and broccoli.

<u>B complex</u>: Leafy green vegetables and green fruit.

<u>C</u>: Citrus fruits, red chilli peppers, kale, parsley, cauliflower, broccoli, turnip greens, sprouts, spinach, cabbage, mangoes, oysters, lima beans, strawberries, and raspberries.

<u>E</u>: Vegetable oil, wheat germ, soybeans, whole grains, raw nuts, raw seeds, and eggs.

<u>PABA</u>: Whole grains, eggs, milk, liver, yoghurt, and molasses.

Recommended Daily Health Tip
Take foods or supplement high in Magnesium to help with circulation and nerve pain. Take the supplement at night as it will also help with sleep.

Best Day and Number

Aquarius is ruled by Saturn and Uranus and is governed by Saturday and the number 4.

Mantra

Portable healthy food will keep me going all day.

Personal Notes:

Pisces

February 19th to March 20th

Sign Profile

Pisces are compassionate, psychic, creative, sensitive, ungrounded, vague, indecisive, empathic, artistic, confused, charitable, spiritual, and caring by nature.

Pisces are very sensitive and empathic, easily absorbing whatever energy is in their environment. This energy can be from pollution, food, water, negative people's energy, and chemicals from household products. Pisces need to be very diligent if they wish to be healthy as they have a very delicate body constitution. If they become unwell their immune system will be directly affected.

Ruled by planets Neptune and Jupiter, Pisces has great compassion. This is a wonderful trait that Pisces possess, unfortunately this is also their fatal flaw. They will sacrifice their time, energy, money and home if they believe it will help someone. When they do this constantly, it keeps the person they are 'helping' in victim mode and drains their vital force or 'Chi'. This 'Chi' is directly connected to their immunity, which when compromised can bring disease and fatigue. Strong boundaries and saying 'NO' and meaning it will go a long way in maintaining optimal health.

Pisces has sensitivity over the feet. It is not uncommon to have bunions, fallen arches, dainty or large feet. Plantar warts reside on the soles of the feet and are largely due to poor immunity. Some suggestions in dealing with plantar warts include: ingesting garlic, applying fresh garlic directly on the plantar wart, applying essential tea tree oil externally, boost your vitamin C intake and the herb Astragalus.

Case Study

Phoebe came to see me complaining of body weakness, loss of appetite and was recovering from a chest infection. Her doctor had prescribed antibiotics which were working well, but she was still feeling lethargic and tired. I explained that when you are recovering from any illness, it takes a toll on the body and that is normal. In our discussion she mentioned she often got sick and she was sick of being sick all the time. I assessed her astrology chart and saw her Sun was in a difficult aspect to planets Saturn and Neptune which explained her depleted vitality. These planets had been playing havoc in her chart for a few years, so I recommended the following;

The immune system and lymphatics are connected. Toxins sit in your lymphatics and affect your immunity. As the Lymphatic system has NO pump to expel toxins, it needs to be stimulated. Some suggestions are: lymphatic massage, daily exercise, deep breathing through the nostrils, exercise and jumping up and down, as well as:

- Iron tincture
- Add garlic in your diet
- Drink Echinacea tea
- 24-hour Vitamin C with bioflavonoids 2gs daily (powder) and 3gs to be taken in winter
- Check your Vitamin D levels and make sure they are at least at 100 to maintain health
- Lymphatic drainage
- Head and neck exercises for the lymph
- Selenium drops
- Anti-inflammatory diet

Phoebe finished her antibiotics and I recommended she have plain unsweetened yoghurt or probiotics for 2 weeks during and after her treatment. This helps with 'thrush' or Candida Albicans which contributes to fatigue. Once done, she started on the plan I advised. I suggested she stay on this regime as part of her daily routine for life to maintain a strong immunity.

Associated Body Organs

- Lymphatic System
- Immune System
- Body parts affected: feet, toes, immune system, body fluids, spinal fluid, lymphatic system, pineal gland, plasma, and blood.

Other body systems that need support to promote vitality for Pisces sign are, the Autonomic Nervous system, Upper Digestion, Respiratory and the Central Nervous system.

Pisces people know when they are unbalanced because:

Pisceans are known for their compassion and imagination. When unbalanced they can become indecisive, confused, vague, impractical, and hypersensitive. Their lack of personal boundaries with others will either engage them in victim mentally where they feel the 'world owes them' or rescue mentality where they feel they need to 'save everyone'. Neither is healthy. When unsettled they may choose to escape through recreational drugs, excessive shopping, or some other form of addiction just to feel better.

How best to overcome Stress

<u>Minimising Stress</u>
Pisces are very sensitive, and the arts suit them well when it comes to relaxation. They enjoy writing poetry, painting, watching sad movies, listening to music, nature, photography, sculpture, and dance. Their home environment and surroundings need to be serene to soothe their receptive nature. Having a flowing water feature in the home also helps as water and rain soothes their soul. Being grounded is also important for them, so having strong feminine wood furniture in their home helps achieve this. Meditation in a peaceful place calms your mind and connects you to spirit.

Pisces love spas and all water sports like surfing, swimming, diving, rowing, rafting, and fishing. Gymnastics, ice skating, Yoga, Tai Chi, and dancing also work well for you. Avoid dark blue and black as they promote depression. Wear more greens, yellows, and earth colours.

Therapies that benefit you include foot reflexology, float tanks, anything mystic, homeopathy, and lymphatic drainage.

Recommended Therapies

Aromatherapy

<u>Signature Oil - Melissa</u>
Melissa oil is an antidepressant; it is antiseptic, meditative, calmative and a stimulant. Brings about a peaceful state, encouraging strength and revitalisation.

Ayurveda

<u>Dosha Constitution</u> - Kapha/Vata, the water and air elements. Primarily rules feet, toes, body fluids, lymphatic and immune system.

Bach Flowers

<u>Pisces - Rock Rose</u>
Associated with extreme fear and at times terror. Easily frightened by life resulting in panic, fear, and anxiety. Very sensitive and connected to the esoteric realms. Rock Rose will help bring in the creative and empathic side, finding the courage to trust in life and themselves.

Chakra

<u>Spiritual Chakra - Svadhisthana</u>
Correlates to the second chakra in the sacral area, this is primarily concerned with linking you to your creative side intuitively with wisdom. Due to their sensitive natures, intimate contact with these people should be sacred as they seek union on a spiritual level and have problems with boundaries.

Signs of imbalance: lower back pain, reproductive complaints, bladder, kidney troubles, unbalanced sex drive, guilt, feelings of isolation and emotional instability.

Colour

<u>TURQUOISE</u> - the colour of calm and confidence

Positive - refreshing, clear, youthful, sensitive, transformational
Negative - confused, unimaginative, uncertain, disturbed, dull

Balance negative vibrations by using brown, purple, pink and dark blue.

Affirmation- 'I am becoming more creative, imaginative and transformational in my work.'

Crystals

<u>Amethyst</u> - promotes peace and serenity. Works well in physical, psychological, and emotional pain issues. Ideal for meditation and attuning to psychic ability. Clears and stabilises the aura.

Physically works well relieving anger, rage, fear, and anxiety. Supports the endocrine, immune, respiratory, and psychiatric systems.

Herbs

- Astragalus, an immune stimulant
- Bilberry, an antioxidant herb
- Chamomile calms nerves
- Dandelion to release accumulated fluid in the body
- Echinacea to support the immune system
- Garlic as a natural antimicrobial

It is highly recommended that you consult a Naturopath or Herbalist if you choose to use herbs. Some herbs may be contraindicated with prescribed medicines. The safest way to use fresh herbs is as a brewed tea or in cooking.

Minerals

Pisces are compassionate, sensitive, psychic, introverted, artistic, escapist, co-dependent, kind, self-sacrificing, empathic, and moody. Due to having difficulty in maintaining boundaries with others, they can take on their mental and emotional traumas that deplete their energy. Prone to feet disorders, gout, chilblains, low immunity, colds, sluggish lymphatic, water retention, allergies, and low metabolism.

Essential minerals - zinc, iron, copper

Enriched food sources-oysters, lean red meat, peanuts, dairy, sardines, dark leafy green vegetables, nuts, seeds, cocoa, mushroom, and whole grain cereals.

Nutrition

Pisces rules the immune and lymphatic system, feet, toes, pineal gland, body fluids and blood. Common ailments include swollen lymph glands, colds, flu, fatigue, alcoholism, weak lungs, foot problems, poor circulation, gout, irregular white cell count, viral and bacterial infections, immune infections, autoimmune disorders, and mucosal discharges.

Beneficial foods includes, ginger, onion, berries, beans, dates, figs, spinach, citrus fruit, green leafy veggies, parsley, raisins, spinach, nuts, molasses, legumes, egg yolk, leafy green veggies, kelp, pumpkin seeds and wheat germ; tomato, apricots and peaches, liquids such as water, veggie juice, herbal teas, soup, a little freshly squeezed fruit juice is OK. Avoid stimulants, alcohol, drugs, and overeating.

Tissue Salt

Iron Phosphate is also known as Ferrum Phos.

When lacking Iron phosphate Pisces will exhibit dizziness, malaise, fever, spontaneous nosebleeds, inflammation, pallor, blurred vision, chronic conditions, anaemia and sensitive to noise and cold.

Foods containing iron phosphate include cabbage, cucumbers, almonds, lima beans, spinach, lentils, barley, radishes, horseradish, potato skins, pumpkin, walnuts, apples, dates, and strawberries.

Vitamins

Foods containing essential vitamins suitable for Pisces:

<u>A:</u>   Liver, carrots, parsley, sweet potato, spinach, mangoes, chives, tomatoes and broccoli.

<u>B complex:</u>   Leafy green vegetables and green fruit.

<u>C:</u>   Citrus fruits, red chilli peppers, kale, parsley, cauliflower, broccoli, turnip greens, sprouts, spinach, cabbage, mangoes, oysters, lima beans, strawberries, and raspberries.

<u>D:</u>   Fish liver oils, tuna, salmon, sardines, seaweeds, and dairy.

> **Recommended Daily Health Tip**
> Have long acting Vitamin C daily as this will help support your immune system

Best Day and Number

Pisces is ruled by Jupiter and Neptune and is governed by Thursday and the number 3.

Mantra

My boundaries are strong and NO means Not On.

Personal Notes:

For the Advanced Astrologer

Since the release of *Learn to Self Heal* in 2018, some of my colleagues have approached me saying my book is too simplistic in its approach.

I explained my intention of *Learn to Self Heal* was to create an easy to read book, packed with information relating to health.

It was written as an introductory book, aimed at those who have little or no knowledge around Medical Astrology, Ayurveda, or Spiritual health. As a health book, it was designed to give options to those who seek alternative choices.

In the spirit of ongoing education and knowledge, I dedicate this section to all Astrologers who choose to incorporate Medical Astrology in their practice.

First, I wish to mention how Medical Astrology can be used to benefit your client.

What Medical Astrology reveals:

- Highlights health and body weakness in the natal chart which when triggered can bring symptoms and/or illness.
- Helps to determine lunar fertility times for pregnancy.
- Establishes the best surgery times to minimise post-operative complications.
- Can reveal ideals modes of treatment and therapy suited to the individual.
- Can identify appropriate foods and diet for the constitution.
- Can identify vitamins and minerals that need replacement.
- Can determine the length of an illness.

- Will identify psychological patterns of behaviour that contribute to dis-ease.
- Can foresee times of vitality and times of stress.
- Can look at family genetics.
- Working the crosses can reveal and heal ailments.
- Working with the elements helps to establish balance for health.

If you package this information in an appealing manner, this can be an excellent marketing tool in attracting clients.

I will be going over my process in how I assess a birth chart with a medical/health focus. I will not be analysing any health conditions, as they are already outlined in my book *Learn to Self Heal* and covered under the 'Sun Sign' section of this book. Detecting diseases astrologically will be covered in a follow-up book *Astrological Signatures of Disease*.

I use Astrological Methodology in assessing a chart to highlight potentials for disease. I recommend being proactive with body maintenance and living life with psycho-spiritual awareness to minimise disease onset.

My assessment process comes in 5 stages.

1. The Client
2. The Chart
3. Body Balance
4. Recommendations
5. Follow up

Stage 1. The Client

Investing in your health secures your future and your wealth.

The client is a very important part of the process. I know this may seem obvious, but as Astrologers, we sometimes get lost in the astrology process and negate what the client actually needs.

Step 1. Always ask the client why they are seeking a session at this time and what they expect as an outcome.

In my experience clients usually come when they are in crisis and are seeking answers.

Listen very carefully to their response and write it down word for word. This is very important as it gives clues to what you need to be looking for in the chart.

As an example, a client states they have an ongoing infection that they cannot get rid of. So, the clues are: (1) infection, rulership is planets Mars or Pluto; (2) ongoing, so it is chronic in nature. Look to planets Saturn, Neptune and of course the client's Sun sign and ascendant. Have a quick look at how these planets are relating to each other in the client's birth chart and by transit to see if there is a dynamic that is playing out. Sometimes it is very clear and other times you need to investigate further. This is why a full client questionnaire is vital.

The Questionnaire

My questionnaire is very extensive. This comes from my vast experience as a Registered Nurse. It has given me the understanding that a complete client history is invaluable as a tool in health assessment. The more information you have, the more thorough you are in delivering what the client needs for good health. This information is a guide only. You (the practitioner) will develop your own questionnaire form depending on your requirements and experience.

Questionnaire Form

-Name

-Date, time and city of birth

-Contact details (phone and/or email)

-Description of their condition, signs and symptoms, diagnosis by any health professional, what part of their body is affected and when was the first onset of condition (month and year).

-Any information about operations (surgery) or if they have had this condition before.

-How many hours sleep they get at night; do they fall asleep easily and do they wake feeling refreshed in the morning?

-How regular are their bowels, do their stools sink or float, and are they fully formed? Also is their flatus offensive (in smell) when passed?

-What colour is their tongue first thing in the morning before tea, food, cigarettes or mouth care? (If possible, please send a photo to practitioner's phone for a tongue assessment)

-What are the stressors in their life and how do they usually deal with stress?

-What do they do for fun and how often?

-How would they rate their energy levels out of 10 with 10 being the highest?

-How much exercise do they do a week, honestly?

-Describe a weekly meal plan and state how many times a week they eat takeaway.

-How many litres of fluid does the client drink daily, excluding coffee and alcohol?

-How much coffee and alcohol do they drink weekly?

-Do they have a sweet tooth?

-Do they smoke and if so, how many per day?

-List of all medications and supplements they are on.

-Are they allergic to anything (including food and medications)? If so, at what age did the allergy start?

-Request a brief medical history of their parents and grandparents on both sides.

-Have they have had any of the following and if so when and what is the name or symptoms of the ailment?

- Blood disorders
- Constipation
- Diarrhoea
- Digestive disturbance
- Dizziness
- Endocrine problems (which glands)
- High or low blood pressure
- Headaches
- Heart problems
- Menstrual or menopause problems
- Nervous disorders
- Pregnant
- Urinary discomfort

- Sugar cravings and if so what time of day?

- Any pain? What part of the body and for how long?

- Request a copy of any relevant current blood tests.

- What was their last Vitamin D level and when was it taken?

- Are all their personal and professional relationships happy?

This assessment of the client is more than helpful, it is important. As you know the body systems are linked, just like they are in a car. If one system is faulty it can affect the function of other systems connected to it. Like a car, the body functions well when all systems work well together. These questions help me decipher what is going on with the person and guides me through the chart process.

Stage 2. The Chart

Once I have read the questionnaire and underlined key words and dates, I then assess the chart. Now the investigation begins.

Elements

I first count up the elemental attributes in the chart. I give 3 points for Sun, Moon and Ascendant; 2 points for personal planets; 1 point for outer planets. This shows me strengths and weakness in the body constitution. This information is used when I look at body balance which I will explore in more depth below.

Planets

I then look at all the planets to see what condition they are in. If planets are in fall or detriment, aspecting the Sun, Moon or ascendant, then these could be troublesome for the person. Planets in strong condition by rulership or exaltation are areas of strength, even if they have difficult aspects. Strong condition shows there is an ability to overcome the disease. Likewise, if planets are in fall or detriment, then there may be trouble in overcoming the illness, so diligent care is needed here.

I take particular note of the luminaries and ascendant and if they are in challenging aspects by birth and/or transit.

The following defines what each planet rules:

Sun – Vitality: the heart, hyper/hypothermia, vision, right eye of men and left eye of women, self-esteem, cell nucleus, consciousness, creativity.

Moon - Nutritive: body cycles, body fluids, feeding patterns, fertility, lactation, habits, right eye in women and left eye in men, limbic system, circadian rhythms, lymphatic system, emotional illness, eating disorders, water retention, vomiting, digestion disorders, memory and soul expression.

Mercury - Neural: respiratory, hearing, mental processing, verbal skills, manual dexterity, nervous disorders - both mental and physical, coordination problems.

Venus - Lymphatic: glandular, homeostasis, kidneys, hormones, veins, venereal disease, bladder disorders, diabetes, sugar cravings, cysts, benign tumours.

Mars - Inflammatory: acute, muscles, adrenals, body heat, libido, haemoglobin, iron, immunity, fevers, burns, wounds, cuts, surgery, skin eruptions.

Jupiter - Liver: fat metabolism, stroke, hyperglycaemia, locomotor disorders, benign tumours.

Saturn - Restrictive: chronic, skeletal, skin, teeth, sclerosis (hardening) of tissues, atrophy, spleen, stiffness, deafness, depression, Parkinson disease, deformity, chills.

Uranus - Spasmodic: electric, disruptive, shock, cramps, ruptures, heart arrhythmias, ADHD, autism, Asperger's, lack of coordination.

Neptune - Dissolution: membrane permeability, pineal gland, allergies, addictions, auto-immune disease, fungal/viral disease, Chronic Fatigue Syndrome, poisoning, lethargy, coma, altered states, drugs, misdiagnosis, Alzheimer's disease, psychic disorders.

Pluto - Eliminatory: transformative, regeneration, birth, death, abscess, malignancies, toxicity, fistulas.

Transpluto - linked to auto-immune conditions. Transpluto in challenging aspects can indicate a person who suppresses their emotions. The native is literally attacking themselves which is how an auto-immune condition is classified. Research into this has been done by Medical Astrologer Lynn Koiner.

Signs

Aries has rulership over the Muscular System. Body parts related to Aries are the head, eyes, nose, brain, pituitary and adrenal glands. Also, blood, iron, and vitality.

Taurus has rulership over the Metabolic System. Body parts related to Taurus are throat, tonsils, neck, ears, vocal cords, jaw, teeth, shoulders, cervical region, and thyroid gland.

Gemini has rulership over the Central Nervous and Respiratory system. Body parts related to Gemini are shoulders, arms, hands, lungs, thymus, bronchi, and respiration. Also nerves and their connections and oxygenation of the blood.

Cancer has rulership over the Lower Digestive System. Body parts related to Cancer are breast, stomach uterus, bile, lymph, and saliva. Also, mucus membranes e.g. pleural cavity.

Leo has rulership over the Cardiac system. Body parts related to Leo are heart, spine, spleen, thoracic and bone marrow.

Virgo has rulership over the Upper Digestion. Body parts related to Virgo are small intestines, solar plexus and pancreas, nerves, and nutrient assimilation.

Libra has rulership over the Endocrine system. Body parts related to Libra are kidneys, bladder, ureters, ovaries, and lumbar region. Also, acid/alkaline balance and hormones.

Scorpio has rulership over the Reproductive and Elimination systems. Body parts related to Scorpio are sex organs, anus, urethra, bladder, bone marrow, colon, and nose. Also, detoxification and sweat.

Sagittarius has rulership over the Autonomic Nervous System. Body parts related to Sagittarius are thighs, hips, liver, sciatic nerve, and pancreas. Also rules coordination and locomotion.

Capricorn has rulership over the Skeletal System. Body parts related to Capricorn are bone, teeth, skin, hair, knees, joints, tendons, nails, gallbladder, and structure.

Aquarius has rulership over the Circulatory system. Body parts related to Aquarius are skin, shins, ankles, and calves. Also, varicose veins, nerve transmission and spasms.

Pisces has rulership over the Immune and Lymphatic system. Body parts related to Pisces are feet, toes, ears, eyes, lymph nodes, blood cells, and pineal gland. Also rules blood for the immune system.

Aspects

I look for all the astrological aspects that may cause imbalance.

Aspects primarily used in Medical Astrology are the *conjunction* giving an intense condition; *sextiles* and *trines* that show ease of the energy; *squares* and *opposition* that give frustrating and conflicting energy and the *quincunx* which will show adjustments are needed in life to bring balance to the condition. There are others, but for the purpose of this book I will follow the main 6 aspects.

The *Yod* is the most difficult aspect to work with in Medical Astrology.

There are 2 quincunxes as part of a Yod. You need to assess the 3 points and the opposition of the apex when establishing imbalance and suggested treatment. When the Yod is activated by transit it activates the whole Yod. This is why many people with this configuration have chronic conditions and healing takes time.

The same principle applies to the *square* and *T-square*. With the T-square, you need to support all aspects of that T-square. The empty leg is usually where symptoms or disease will manifest if you do not manage the T-square well. The empty leg is like a dumping ground.

For example: if someone has a cardinal T-square and the empty leg is Aries, then the person may exhibit signs and symptoms of headaches, adrenal exhaustion, or muscle pain. Address the Signs on the cross. For the sign Cancer, investigate how the person's digestion and correct it. In Libra make sure their fluid intake is high to promote good kidney function. Coffee and alcohol are not counted in the fluid total as they are both dehydrating in nature. In Capricorn if fluid intake is low then there is a build-up of uric acid which cannot be excreted. This contributes to bone issues like gout and arthritis resulting from faulty digestion. All these elements contribute to the Aries condition and need to be rectified for good health. Cardinal-cross people are good at getting things done, a plan of action in conjunction with health professionals will work well.

Houses

Houses of potential illness in astrology are, the 1st which is the physical body, the 4th the end of the matter, the 6th house of acute and digestion, the 8th house of genetics and transformation, and the 12th house of hospitals and chronic illness. Any aspects connecting these houses are of significance and should be investigated. Do not dismiss planets in other houses.

Below is an outline of each of the houses in relation to body dynamics.

First

Your Vitality, physical appearance, condition at birth, head, brain, muscular system.

Second

Throat, neck, Chi movement, lymphatics, metabolic system.

Third

Nerves, arms, hands, learning disabilities, central nervous system.

Fourth

Stomach, breasts, childhood trauma, inherited medical issues, lower digestive system.

Fifth

Heart, spine, pregnancy, liver, heart chakra, cardiac system.

Sixth

Intestines, upper digestive system, acute illness, congenital health issues, diet, daily health routines.

Seventh

Kidneys, lower back, homeostasis, endocrine system.

Eighth

Colon, sex organs, deep healing, reproductive system.

Ninth

Hips, thighs, autonomic system.

Tenth

Skin, knees, bones, skeletal system.

Eleventh

Circulation, legs, calves, circulatory system.

Twelfth

Feet, chronic illness, karmic illness, lymphatic system, immune system.

Transit

Assessing the current transit and progressions are next. As we know a transit is a trigger. It will spark off an event in the chart and this is also true for disease. All the rules of transits apply here. Applying transits to any planet has the strongest influence; once past, and separating by 1-2 degrees of orb, the illness starts to subside. This may take years if outer planets are involved or if a Stellium or Yod is being activated in the chart.

Check out midpoints in the chart. Although not obvious when assessing the chart, midpoints often come into play.

The main midpoints to consider are

- Sun/Moon
- Saturn/Mars
- Saturn/Neptune
- Saturn/Pluto

Look to midpoints depending on the nature of the illness. For spasm or palpitations, you would include planets Mercury and Uranus in your analysis. Likewise, if you were looking for fertility questions you would include the Moon and Venus in your assessment.

Psychological Factors

Discomfort in the body which leads to disease does not happen by itself. It usually takes time. Yes, there can be an astrological health challenge in the chart, but this is usually backed up with a psychological conditioning, usually from childhood. This conditioning is usually a pattern of behaviour that is unconscious to the person. This behaviour is like a bad habit that in time will contribute to, and in some cases cause an imbalance in the body leading to dis-ease. It is usually at this time they seek out medical or health professionals looking for answers and hopefully a cure.

Your role as an astrologer can be very helpful here. You can help and support your clients by identifying the psychological challenges which may be contributing to their condition.

An example, anyone who has malefic planets, Mars and Saturn in aspect, will experience frustration which can bring on temper. Frustration causes stress in the body and this will raise cortisol levels. This increases heat in the body providing a perfect environment for parasites, bacteria, and viruses to grow. Have you ever wondered why operating theatres in hospitals are so cold? It is simple, bugs cannot survive in this cool environment.

When it comes to the body, anyone with anger issues will have a body high in heat and/or high in acid. This will result in an increased risk of infections and inflammatory conditions during their lifetime.

Best practice is to avoid eating heat inducing foods and stop engaging in adrenaline type activities. Having an alkaline or anti-inflammatory diet, with lots of water to prevent dehydration, helps to reduce inflammation in the body and keep the body in harmony with itself. Being self-aware and identifying triggers that spark off frustration is proactive and healthy. Dealing with anger (passive or external) in a functional manner is far more productive for healing. As the liver is the seat of anger, regular liver support and liver cleanses are advised.

Other Considerations

Critical Degrees

Critical degrees are an ancient system which was primarily used in Medical Astrology. These degrees when transited by the moon can predict the progress of an illness. Days on which the moon passes over these critical degrees is known as *critical degree days* and can indicate a change in the course of events.

In natal astrology, a planet within a 2-3-degree orb of the critical degree is known to have the energy of exaltation.

- Angular houses and planets on either side by an orb of 2 degrees are significant. The critical degrees of the qualities are as follows;

- Cardinal degrees 13 and 26

- Fixed degrees 9 and 12

- Mutable degrees 4 and 17

- Also 29 and 00 degrees of all the signs

Note how most antibiotics scripts are for 7 days (one lunar phase) and there is an expected change in health at that time. This is why medical practitioners advise you to take the full course of antibiotics and not stop when *you feel better*. If on antibiotics, make sure you ingest plain natural yoghurt high in Acidophilus. This will prevent the onset of oral and digestive Candidiasis or most commonly known as Thrush.

Stage 3. Body Balance

Once the planetary assessments are completed, the next step is to look at how to bring the body back to balance.

As mentioned earlier 3 points are given for Sun, Moon and Ascendant, 2 points for personal planets, 1 point for outer planets. This shows strengths and weakness in the body constitution. I assess their elements and qualities with this process.

Elements

AIR - Related to the signs Gemini, Libra and Aquarius.

Has body rulership over the central nervous system, respiratory, endocrine, and circulatory systems.

Air is essential for movement, connection, and flow within the body.

When balanced there is a style and beauty in movement, they communicate well with others and have an accurate perception of the world.

WHEN IN EXCESS OF AIR YOU EXHIBIT

-restlessness, agitation, scattered, nervousness and jittery behaviour

-rough skin, brittle hair, and nails due to dryness

-stiff joints

-flatulence, asthma, and nervous disorders

-may appear aloof and detached in nature

-over stimulation of ideas bring lack of focus

TO BALANCE

-due to dehydration and dryness you need extra fluids to nourish your organs and regular oil massage

-outdoor activities promotes air circulation, swimming promotes hydration, walking gives grounding and meditation to calms the mind

-add whole grains, green leafy veggies, and root veggies to your diet for grounding

-add vitamin B complex, magnesium, calcium and manganese and good fish oils to calm your nerves

- add cooking herbs cinnamon, fennel, cumin, cardamom, and warm milk

-nervine herbs such as valerian, hops, skullcap, chamomile, Ashwagandha, Brahmi and Gotu Kola to calm nerves

-wear colours green, violet and browns and aromatherapy oils lavender, rose and sandalwood to calm and ground you

-avoid coffee, chocolate, and cocoa as these stimulate the nervous system and alcohol as this act a diuretic causing further dehydration

WHEN LACKING IN AIR YOU EXHIBIT

-tiredness, shortness of breath, feelings of introversion

-slow movements and unable to coordinate freely

-shallow breathing

-unable to perceive things as they really are

-weakness in the nervous system

-difficulty in communicating easily

TO BALANCE

-deep breathing exercises in the form of pranayama, nostril breathing, yoga, dance, tai chi, martial arts especially aikido to enable body coordination and breath awareness

-networking with groups helps to facilitate communication skills

-learn to play a wind instrument

-aromatherapy oil rosemary to help stimulate memory

-Brahmi, Gotu Kola and Gingko to support the memory and nerves

-wear more blues to stimulate mental activity

-nervine herbs to support the nerves such as valerian, hops, skullcap, and chamomile

-add vitamin B complex, magnesium, calcium, and manganese to support nerves

FIRE - Related to the signs Aries, Leo and Sagittarius.

Has body rulership over the muscular, cardiac, and autonomic nervous systems.

Fire is essential for vitality, digestion and promotes passion and action.

When balanced they have ample energy, are inspirational, affectionate, self-confidant, positive and can manifest ideas into action.

WHEN IN EXCESS OF FIRE YOU EXHIBIT

-prone to anger, frustration, violent and/or aggressive behaviour

-rashness, impulsive behaviour

-prone to liver and digestive problems, ulcers, gallbladder disease, infections, inflammation of the skin which includes redness of the face

-adrenal exhaustion

-excess perspiration

-dehydration and dryness

TO BALANCE

-add more fluids to replenish body fluids, extra in summer

-include swimming and avoid hot showers in your daily routine

-avoid acid forming foods which increase heat in the body

-eat more cooling foods e.g. salads, fruits and add Aloe Vera juice to cool the body

-wear blues and greens to cool the body and if quick to anger use chamomile and lavender to calm

-avoid sugar and spices, peppers, chili, and curry which are heating as well as coffee and alcohol which promotes dehydration causing dryness

-use coconut oil as massage and in diet your which is cooling by nature

-minimise exposure to the sun and wear a hat in hot weather

-liver detox in Spring and Autumn

WHEN LACKING IN FIRE YOU EXHIBIT

-cold feet and hands from poor circulation

-poor muscle tone and stiffness in the body

-low vitality and indigestion

-lack of confidence, motivation, and courage

-unable to assimilate food therefore inadequate fuel resources for energy which will manifest as fatigue and vagueness

-toxins are on the increase due to the body is unable to digest food

TO BALANCE

-aerobic exercise to increase circulation and tone the body

-hiking and mountain climbing to promote self-confidence

-warming spices like cayenne, cinnamon, cardamom, and curry to help stimulate heat in the body

-digestive bitters help to digest toxins

-warm water and lemon juice in the morning and herbal teas to help digest toxins e.g. ginger and peppermint

-wear red, orange and yellow clothes promote confidence and motivation

-aromatherapy black pepper, basil and cinnamon promote the fire element

WATER - Related to the signs Cancer, Scorpio and Pisces.

Has body rulership over the lower digestion, reproductive, lymphatic, and immune systems

Water is essential cleansing and nourishing the body organs

When balanced they relate well emotionally, are empathic, creative, and intuitive.

WHEN IN EXCESS OF WATER YOU EXHIBIT

-issues with excess weight, slow to move, drowsy and self-indulgent

-over emotional, security conscious, live in a dream like state

-accumulate mucus in the body, prone to colds and lymph congestion

-unable to maintain and distinguish healthy boundaries in relationships

-too much of a giver but not good at receiving

-cares for others more and lacks self-care

TO BALANCE

-eat cooked spicy foods with herbs ginger, black pepper, cayenne, honey

-avoid overeating, having a late dinner, sweet, sour, and salty foods.

-drink diuretic teas such as dandelion, nettle and alfalfa

-avoid cold foods and dairy as it slows the circulation and causes blockage. This includes ice.

-if you drink milk heat it first to change its constitution from heavy to light so it easier to digest

-drink warm fluids over cold fluids

-limit fruit intake as they are primarily water and sugar

-acupuncture or acupressure unblocks channels to allow flow

WHEN LACKING IN WATER YOU EXHIBIT

-lacking in moisture in the body, makes you prone to dehydration, cracks on the skin and lips, rough tight skin, and dryness

-due to lack of lubrication you will have stiff joints and body stiffness

-prone to thirst from dehydration

-may appear older than your years due to your organs being dehydrated

-may suffer the insomnia

-difficulty in verbally expressing emotions, unable to demonstrate feelings of affection and lacks empathy

TO BALANCE

-drink more vegetable juice and herb teas

-add cooling foods to your diet such as melons, grapes, cabbage, lettuce, cucumber and zucchini

-minimise salt and spices as they tend to dry you out

-increase your intake of water to help detoxify and eliminate waste

-take liver tonics to assist in flushing your system e.g. St. Mary's thistle, iris, gentian, and globe artichoke

-live near water or bring a water influence into your home e.g. aquarium

-commence art or music classes to help connect to your intuitive side

-always state what you feel

-wear pastel colours and blues

EARTH-Related to the signs Taurus, Virgo and Capricorn.

Has body rulership over the metabolic, upper digestive and skeletal systems.

Earth is essential for cohesion, grounding, and connection between body organs.

When balanced they are grounded, responsible, nurturing, caring and practical.

WHEN EXCESS IN EARTH YOU EXHIBIT

-will feel lethargic, sluggish, and heavy

-will feel insensitive to others and prone to depression at times

-will lack motivation especially with exercise

-will be over concerned with materialism

-will be introverted and introspective

-will be unable to perceive new ideas quickly

TO BALANCE

-include spices such as cayenne, ginger, cinnamon, black pepper, fenugreek, cumin, and chili which help to create more fire

-avoid overeating, late dinner, sweet, sour, and salty foods

-wear colours yellow and orange to motivate and increase confidence, also wear lapis lazuli necklace or blue scarfs to keep this area of your body open and healthy

-commence an exercise routine e.g. 20 mins walk twice daily

-eat small meals six times a day to help increase metabolism

-limit heavy meats in your diet as they are difficult to digest especially if you have a sluggish metabolism

-would benefit from 5 HTP OR St John's wort at night to promote serotonin levels. (look at natural treatment for depression in my book *Learn to Self Heal*) Make sure there are no interactions with other medications or herbs consult a Naturopath first

-make sure you always speak what you say otherwise internalizing your communications can bring on throat, thyroid and neck issues

-to keep your throat and your ability to communicate exactly what you feel, sing in the car or in the shower as if there is no tomorrow. Have a song that is your philosophy in life and sing it every day

WHEN LACKING IN EARTH YOU EXHIBIT

-often you ignore your own needs

-unable to manifest your own potential

-idealistic, often stuck in your head

- may appear unstable and ungrounded

-unable to focus and maintain direction in your life

-often dreamlike and not in your body

TO BALANCE

-practice grounding techniques e.g. oil massage, walking barefoot on sand or grass, outdoor exercise, martial arts, yoga, and dance as a steady practical routine. Play with young children.

-use aromatherapy sandalwood, cedarwood, angelica, clary sage, lemongrass, rose, sage, and vetiver

-use whole grains and root vegetables e.g. potatoes, carrot, turnips, kumara and pumpkin

-Eat red foods e.g. beetroot, tomato, red apples, strawberry, cherries, plums, watermelon, red kidney beans, red lentils, radishes, and raspberries

-wear reds to motivate, green to balance and brown to ground the body

-eat regular meals to maintain blood sugar levels which keep you focused, do not to skip meals

-rub sesame oil on head and feet to anchor spirit to the body

Qualities

The word quality refers to classification of temperament or character of the person. It also refers to the natal chart and the division of masculine versus feminine signs as this would affect your nature and gives more information on your medical circumstances. They are divided into three types,

Cardinal that is action orientated, dutiful and responsible

Fixed that is stable, focused, and dependable

Mutable that is flexible, adaptable and at times scattered.

CARDINAL QUALITY Aries, Cancer, Libra and Capricorn

Affected body systems include muscular, digestive, endocrine, renal, skeletal, and skin. Cardinal power assists in providing mental energy for the body.

TO BALANCE EXCESS

-practice meditation and self-reflection in order to maintain mental stillness

-daily practice of Yoga or Tai Chi to maintain discipline and balance

-Pranayama or nasal deep breathing

-amethyst and fluorite crystals to aid self-awareness

TO BALANCE LACK

-need to network and get themselves out into the world

-to be physically active e.g. running, team sports and martial arts especially aikido

-wear reds, oranges, and yellows to energise and motivate

-crystals that stimulate energy and grounding include jasper, ruby, red carnelian, hematite, and bloodstone

FIXED QUALITY Taurus, Leo, Scorpio and Aquarius

Affected body systems include throat, thyroid gland, elimination and reproductive organs, the heart, lower back, and circulation of the body. Fixed signs can refer to illnesses that are slow to manifest and are chronic in nature which can last a long time. They do well with intensive therapies.

TO BALANCE EXCESS

-you require strong body therapies to unlock and release physical tensions e.g. oil massage, Bowen therapy, rebirthing, and acupuncture on a weekly basis

-deep physiological therapies which identify old destructive behaviour patterns which no longer benefit you and may be the cause of disease

-crystals snowflake obsidian and smoky quartz for grounding

-add CQ10 and iodine to diet

-low fat low salt diet (sea salt or Himalayan salt is best)

TO BALANCE LACK

-daily physical exercise that provides grounding e.g. outdoor rock climbing, running, team sports and swimming

-commencing projects and follow through till completion

-crystals tiger's-eye and hawk's-eye to assist in keeping energy in the body

-eating of grains and root vegetables e.g. pumpkin, carrot, turnips, and potato to ground and integrate energy

MUTABLE QUALITY Gemini, Virgo, Sagittarius and Pisces

Affected body systems include central nervous, digestion, immune and the liver. Mutable power assists in providing motivated energy to the body.

TO BALANCE EXCESS

-exercises like Yoga, martial arts, walking on grass or sand, and tai chi to facilitate grounding and discipline

-eating red foods and wearing red socks and under garments for grounding

-energetic therapies to balance chakras

-eating small meals every 3 hours to fuel the mind and maintain focus

-gemstones for grounding are aventurine, green calcite, malachite and chrysoprase

TO BALANCE LACK

-maybe very rigid in their mental, emotional, and physical attitudes

-prone to body stiffness so regular warm oil massage is beneficial

-needs to learn to flow so dance and swimming will assist in this

-crystals like rose quartz, kunzite and sugilite assists in promoting flow

Stage 4. Recommendations

With recommendations, start with what a client will do. For example, if a parent has 3 preschool kids at home and wants to lose weight, saying they need to go to the gym every day is not productive. Playing soccer with her kids in the park would be better and more beneficial. The message here is, I always start with what the client can control and for most people this is the diet.

Ayurveda has always known that digestive fire (Agni) is the seat of disease and needs to be strong for optimal health. Incomplete bowel evacuation, bloating, irregular bowel habits and offensive flatus are signs of a disturbed digestion. This needs to be corrected before you can look at any other healing practices. Whatever happens in the digestion will feed the whole body.

Depending on the condition of the client's digestion, I may recommend a combination of the following;

- parasite cleanse
- probiotics
- high fibre diet
- more exercise
- tongue scraping
- digestive herbs
- alkaline diet
- extra fluids
- digestive enzymes
- lemon water in morning

If there is heat, redness, inflammation, or pain in the body, then the liver needs to be addressed. The liver and digestion work together to breakdown food to remove toxins from the body. They work as a team. If either the digestion or liver are disturbed, then both need to be brought back into healthy balance to promote optimal function.

Recommendations for the liver include;

-liver cleanse in spring and Autumn

-liver support herbs

-dandelion coffee

-low fat, low meat diet

-drink more water

-fluid fast 1 day a week

-alkaline diet

-warm lemon water in the morning

-deal with anger issues in a proactive manner

-have coconut water and cook with coconut oil

-avoid omega 6 oils as they cause inflammation. Use more omega 3 oils as they reduce inflammation.

Supporting and bringing both digestion and liver function back to balance is the foundation for healing in the body. (There is a whole section on digestive health in my book *Learn to Self Heal*).

Stage 5. The Follow-up

Once the client has left with their plan of action, and if there is no follow-up appointment scheduled, I recommend an email or phone call about one week later. Book a time that is suitable for both of you and ask them to have any questions ready for you to answer.

Limit the time to thirty minutes. This is usually enough time to discuss any concerns and short enough that it will not impede your time or your clients. As an incentive I offer the thirty-minute follow-up service included in the consultation fee. Since the client has already paid for it, the appointment is usually assured.

It is rare that a client comes to you looking for a health maintenance plan. Most people are not proactive in their health, so you will usually get clients seeking quick results.

It is important to convey to the client that the process of illness usually takes many years to establish. This results from bad habits, both physical, mentally and emotional. Psychological blocks are another reason for disease. These need to be identified and dealt with in order for complete healing to take place.

Bringing balance back to the body and freeing the body from disease with alternative therapies takes time. Adjustment to their daily life, removal of long held beliefs and bad habits, diligent self-care and a strict routine followed by the client. Hard work and patience are needed. Some will fail. Others will succeed. If their need to get well is strong, the client will make a lasting recovery by following your recommendations in cooperation with other health professionals.

Do not let other people's lack of ability with themselves to succeed, affect your capacity as a Medical Astrologer in helping others. You will get many clients who will thank you for your time and efforts.

If assessment of the client reveals they lack discipline to achieve success (look at their Saturn), book weekly consultations until they can manage on their own.

In a Nutshell

- First, I send them a detailed questionnaire to get the relevant and accurate information I need

- Once I have that I then cast the chart and look to see if the chart is in balance with the modes and elements. Giving information here helps to keep the body maintained and balanced

- Next, I write down what the ailment is, along with the signs and symptoms. I note the date and look to see if the astrology correlates

- I then look at the vitality of lord 1, lord 6 the Sun, Moon and Mars and see if they are strong, weak or in aspect

- I listen to the complaint and investigate the house and planets that rules the symptom

- I take a look at the midpoints and critical degrees to see if there are planets triggering the points causing the problem

- Look to see if there are any difficult aspects when it started and for how long

- Recommend solutions based on my knowledge. This may include vibrational treatment, Ayurveda, colour, herbs, vitamin and mineral supplements, types of exercise and food

- If genetic factors are involved (8th house and history) and there is a signature in the chart I strongly recommend strengthening those areas

- I may recommend blood tests

- I marry the symptom with Louise Hay's metaphysical meaning from her book **You can Heal your Life**

Live in Full Energy

About the Author

Christina has always had a passion for health and wanting to help others.

Her passion for astrology, combined with her spiritual beliefs, developed her interest in holistic medicine.

Her first book *Learn to Self Heal* has such positive reviews that this led to her second health book *Your Astrological Health*.

A Registered Nurse with many years' experience, she qualified in Indian Ayurveda healing and has, through her own research and practical application, then become aware that the average person's well-being can be maintained, indeed improved, by a range of alternative practices.

She does not discount Western Medicine but believes that in many instances the answers lie elsewhere, and an open mind is crucial to our emotional and physical well-being.

Aware that there was nothing available for the average person to acquaint them with these other beliefs, she has written this book designed to explain other health options and ideologies and provide a detailed description of each. Written in a very easy-to-read style, she has still managed to provide a wealth of knowledge and understanding. So, if your well-being is important to you, you will find this book invaluable reading.

Christina practises worldwide and lives in sunny Hawke's Bay, New Zealand.

She can be contacted at her website: www.christinarichterauthor.com

Acknowledgments

In gratitude and with many thanks...

I would like to acknowledge and express my appreciation to all those people who supported my vision in making this book possible.

First, I would like to give a special thank you my friend and colleague Kath Tutill. Her friendship, solid support and wisdom has been my guiding light and strength.

I also would like to extend my warm appreciation and gratitude to my fellow colleagues Jill Griggs, Phillipa Cummins, Lynn Koiner, Kira Sutherland, and Alan Richards-Wheatcroft. Their contribution has guided my work and I feel blessed to be connected with such esteemed Astrologers.

I wish to thank Win Needham my manuscript assessor from Inklings: Professional Proofreading and editing Services. Without her writing skills and creative computer expertise I could not have completed my vision. To you my friend, my deepest and warmest appreciation.

I personally thank Michele Courage for her inspiration and insight.

Other books by Christina Richter

Learn to Self Heal White Light Publishing

My Fathers Fhilosophy White Light Publishing

Available at www.christinarichterauthor.com

Online Astrology Courses:

Introduction to Astrology 10 Lessons
Level 2 Astrology 10 Lessons

Medical Astrology 101

Medical Astrology 102

Available at:
www.christinarichterauthor.com
www.facebook.com/astropath

 or email me direct on
crscorpio1111@gmail.com

Look out for my next book coming in 2022:
Astrological Signatures of Disease

FREE Astrological Seasonal Newsletter available at
www.christinarichterauthor.com

Learn to Self Heal Reviews

Christina Richter has written an easy to read but comprehensive book, which is filled with valuable information and practical insights. *Learn to Self-Heal* will not only appeal to budding students who wish to convey their knowledge through conventional and alternative means, but it will also be alluring to those who wish to further enhance their overall knowledge of medical astrology. It is a well written book, and it is wonderfully presented — complete with useful tips and empirical suggestions.

I particularly enjoyed the section called 'Modalities of Healing' — containing real life case studies, which highlight the dangers of illness and disease, such as depression. The book touches briefly on the use of conventional medicines, but perhaps more importantly, and for me most impressively, it proposes the use of natural therapies as benevolent attributes towards potential healing. Currently, depression is regarded as one of the most proliferating diseases of today's modern and technological world. Furthermore, the section culminates beautifully with a collective offering of innate and spiritual attributes — denoting the importance of mindfulness, naturopathic medicine, and meditation.

I also enjoyed Christina's recipe ideas — some of which I have adopted. Overall, this is a very knowledgeable book, and within its pages there is no doubt something that will appeal to everyone. *Learn to Self-Heal* is an exceptionally well written book, and it is even in its approach to the practice of medical astrology and all of the disciplines that are connected to and enhanced by it. Therefore, it is a book that I would highly recommend to others. Finally, I feel that this is a book that has been written directly from the *heart*.

Alan Richards-Wheatcroft, Medical Astrologer and Spiritual Healer

Learn to Self-Heal is a book that anyone interested in personal development, astrology, wellness or health should own. It is empowering to say the least!

Personally, I love it because it is easy to read and to the point. You can use this book as an important tool in understanding yourself better as a whole: mind, body, and spirit. But it is also a great aid for astrologers, psychics, healers, teachers, physicians, and nurses.

The book is very well structured with almost surgical precision. You can tell that the author has a solid scientific background that allows her to offer clean-cut information. Despite this type of scientific delivery of information, the book is also very personal, open and humane.

The emphasis is on just what the title says. The metaphysical aspects are there. But not forced on the reader that has total freedom to use the information without directly associating it to a belief system. There is also a great psychological component to the text that I enjoyed and found useful to say the least.

You will also find easy to understand/follow life-style tips and hacks that will help the reader learn how to nurture their body properly and support it in healing the process. Understanding the specific needs of one's ayurvedic body-type brings in ancient wisdom and common sense. This book doesn't sell a quick fix. It offers a new way of understanding and honoring one's self as a unique and complete system. The recommendations are easy to follow and don't encourage absurd or drastic changes making this an encouraging opportunity to take steps in the right direction.

I am sure that Learn to Self-Heal will leave you, as it did me, with all you need to kick start your self-healing journey.

Ioana Dragan, Romania

I have purchased your stunning book and I honestly cannot put it down, it's so extremely fascinating and intriguing to me. I have a lot in common with you and I just wanted to drop you a line to say WOW your book has to be the best book I have ever truly had the pleasure of reading :)

I wanted to personally thank you for sharing your wealth of knowledge with me in your book of "Learn to Self Heal". What an inspirational lady you are and how much I enjoyed meeting you :) From every inch of my soul, Thanks again for such a tremendously exciting, wonderfully written and insightful, helpful Book! Lots of love,

Kristen Johansen, Napier, New Zealand.

White Light
PUBLISHING

www.ingramcontent.com/pod-product-compliance
Lightning Source LLC
Chambersburg PA
CBHW050315010526
44107CB00055B/2246